WILLIAMS-SONOMA

THE NEW SLOW
cooker

RECIPES BRIGIT BINNS

PHOTOGRAPHS KATE SEARS

weldon**owen**

CONTENTS

The New Slow Cook

Slow cookers today remain as popular as they were at their debut some forty years ago, a testament to their versatility, their ease of use, and to the comforting dishes that have impressed home cooks for generations. But today's cooks also want healthy ingredients, fresh flavors, and crunchy textures to be a part of their slow-cooked meals.

When they first appeared in the 1970s, slow cookers were widely promoted as time-savers. The earliest models allowed home cooks to come home after a full day's work and serve a delicious homemade meal that tasted as if they had spent hours stirring a pot on the stove top. Today, the latest generation of slow cookers offers that same appealing convenience, plus new options that expand their versatility beyond what was possible in those early days.

Decades ago, cooks typically tossed a few ingredients into a slow cooker, switched it on, and were content with whatever emerged when the selected time had elapsed. And indeed, without fail, slow cookers still produce fork-tender meat just as they did in the past. But they can also turn out uniformly soft textures, watery flavors, and dull colors, qualities perhaps overlooked in the past in favor of the slow cooker's convenience. Today's cooks—and diners—want more.

In the following pages, you will discover how to ensure your slow-cooked dishes have bright, fresh flavors, colors, and textures. Not only will you understand the importance of selecting the best meats, fish, beans, grains, and vegetables for the slow cooker, but you will also learn how to prepare those ingredients to draw out the most flavor, as well as how to use aromatics, herbs, and garnishes,

salads, or other fresh components to heighten the flavor and appeal of everything you serve. You will also find tips on seasoning for maximum effect, on how to layer ingredients for even cooking, on why browning some ingredients before they go in the cooker contributes more complex flavors, and on how to choose the best slow cooker for your household.

Many of the recipes that follow are innovative updates of classic slow-cooker dishes, such as a meltingly tender beef stew garnished with crisp frisée dressed in a bacon-shallot vinaigrette. Others are brand new, such as a Mediterranean-inspired honey-braised pork loin dressed up with succulent fresh figs, spicy arugula, and crunchy pistachios. Slow cooking recipes often skip fish dishes, but here salmon is simmered with memorable results: the fish, perfumed with herbs, becomes tender and succulent. Vegetables, too, are often ignored, but not in these pages: French ratatouille cooks gently in the steady heat of the slow cooker and emerges with the colors of its summer vegetables still bright and appealing.

All of the recipes in this book deliver the fork-tender texture and kitchen ease that were hallmarks of recipes for early slow cookers. But they are also deliciously contemporary, rich in the robust flavors, crunchy textures, and bright colors of the modern table.

The Benefits of Slow Cooking

Nowadays, home cooks routinely struggle to balance their busy lives with the need to put nutritious, tasty meals on the table. Many of them know that the slow cooker is a time-saver, but they may not know that it is also remarkably versatile and very budget friendly.

Slow cooking has a long history, stretching from the fire pits of prehistoric man to the *cocottes* of twenty-first-century French chefs. This cooking technique exposes food—often tougher cuts of meat—to low temperatures for long periods of time, with moisture playing a critical role, usually through the presence of stock, wine, or other flavorful liquids.

The term *slow* is relative, depending on the main ingredient. For example, for a lamb shank it can mean a full day of simmering. For fish fillets or green vegetables, it may be no more than an hour or two of cooking. The uniform, gentle, moist heat that defines slow cooking can be achieved in a heavy lidded pan—typically a Dutch oven—on the stove top or in the oven. But only an electric slow cooker can consistently and safely hold food at 200°F (95°C) over many hours, rendering meat, poultry, vegetables, dried beans, and grains exquisitely tender and succulent. It offers big rewards for the busy home cook, who can prepare dinner quickly and easily early in the day, leave it to cook unattended while he or she is away, and then serve it hours later for dinner. Plus, many recipes for the slow cooker yield satisfying one-pot meals, removing the need to prepare two or more side dishes to round out the menu.

But the slow cooker offers more than convenience. Even cooks who look forward to—or have the time to—spend hours in the kitchen agree that the results they achieve with a slow cooker are often superior to what they can accomplish with conventional oven or stove top methods. For example, when poultry and meats are braised at the low temperature that is possible in a slow cooker, the natural collagen in their proteins breaks down slowly, resulting in foods that are particularly tender and juicy.

And because the temperature of a slow cooker remains steady, scorching is not a threat and the integrity of the ingredients is maintained: the foods keep their shape, the juices are preserved, and the flavors of the ingredients are pure. The slow cooker is also far more versatile than some cooks realize. In addition to the familiar stews and other braises, it is also ideal for preparing everything from bouillabaisse to polenta to risotto.

Finally, slow cooking is economical cooking. It is perfect for chuck, round, shoulder, shank, ribs, and similar tough cuts whose connective tissue requires low, moist heat for the best flavor and texture. All of them cost a fraction of what their luxury cousins, steaks, tenderloins, and chops, fetch at the butcher shop or supermarket, and they are often just as satisfying. Add color, texture, and flavor with a fresh salsa or relish or a dollop of cool crème fraîche and a sprinkle of fragrant basil or dill, and your penny-wise slow-cooked supper will have everyone at the dinner table asking for seconds.

The Basics

To get the most out of your slow cooker, you will need to spend a little time preparing, seasoning, and layering the ingredients; browning the meat or poultry; and reducing the flavorful braising juices—a handful of simple, quick steps that lead to memorable meals.

SEASONING The first thing that every slow-cooker novice needs to know is that condensation forms on the underside of the lid while the food is cooking. This means that no liquid evaporates, as with many types of conventional cooking, and if not offset some way, it can result in a bland and watery dish. To compensate for the volume of liquid, start with flavorful stocks and/or wine and slightly increase the usual quantities of herbs and spices. If you are adapting a conventional recipe to the slow cooker, reduce the amount of liquid called for in the recipe by half and substitute a full-flavored stock for any water.

PREPARING INGREDIENTS Dense vegetables, such as potatoes, carrots, and other root vegetables, take a long time to become tender in a slow cooker. To ensure they cook through, always cut them into chunks of about 1 inch (2.5 cm) or smaller. Trim as much fat as possible from meat and poultry before you add them to the cooker. This will save you time later when you need to skim the fat off the top of the braising juices. To help them retain their color, blanch assertive greens, such as collards and kale, in boiling water before you add them to the slow cooker.

BROWNING Most recipes that include meat or poultry call for sautéing it in butter or oil to give it a well browned exterior. In the past, slow cooker recipes did not always specify this step, and some busy cooks resist this "extra" task now. Browning,

however, is a crucial flavor-building technique that can make the difference between an insipid result and a deeply flavored dish. Browning also contributes appealing color to a dish.

Nowadays, you can sauté directly in the insert of some slow cookers. If this is true of your model, go ahead and use that feature, instead of the separate pan called for in the recipes in this book. When you are browning the meat or poultry, watch it closely and adjust the heat so the food sizzles steadily but doesn't scorch. You want the entire surface to have a deep, caramelized golden brown hue. The same is true for aromatic vegetables, especially onions, carrots, and celery, which are usually sautéed in the same pan after the protein has been removed.

LAYERING If a recipe calls for dense, firm, or starchy vegetables such as carrots, potatoes, or celery root, be sure to put them into the slow cooker's insert first. Place meat or poultry and more tender vegetables on top. Occasionally, an ingredient will be added after an hour or more of cooking time has elapsed. Follow the recipe directions as to whether the ingredient should be stirred in or layered on top. Fish is often the last item added. In all cases, try to place pieces of the same ingredient in the slow cooker insert in an even layer, so they will cook through at the same rate. When meat, such as beef shanks, must be stacked, arrange them in as few layers as possible.

MAINTAINING THE TEMPERATURE Resist the urge to peek at the cooking food by lifting the lid, unless the directions instruct you to do so. Hot, moist air performs the cooking action, and every time you lift the lid, the slow cooker will take several minutes to return to the right temperature. This can not only affect the cooking time but also compromise safety.

REDUCING Most of the recipes in this book use just enough liquid to create natural, deeply flavored pan juices. They can often be spooned directly onto the dish at serving time to moisten the ingredients and heighten the overall flavor of the dish. However, sometimes you might end up with 2 cups (16 fl oz/ 500 ml) or more of the braising liquid. If this is the case, strain the liquid through a fine-mesh sieve set over a small saucepan, allow it to settle for about 5 minutes, and then skim away the fat from the surface of the liquid using a large metal spoon. Place the saucepan over high heat and boil the liquid to concentrate its flavor and to reduce its volume slightly, usually 5–10 minutes.

CHOOSING A SLOW COOKER

STANDARD SLOW COOKERS

All of the recipes in this book were tested with a 6- or 7-quart (6- or 7-l) slow cooker with a ceramic cooking insert. In most cases, the recipes yield four to six servings, but these larger slow cookers can usually handle recipes that yield double that amount. (The exceptions are recipes that call for cuts with large bones, such as beef, lamb, or veal shanks, which cannot be doubled with great success.) If you double the weight of a large piece of meat, be sure to add an additional 1 to 1½ hours to the cooking time, to ensure the foods cook through properly. If you double the amount of cubed meat or poultry parts, the cooking time will remain the same as in the original recipe.

ALUMINUM INSERTS

Many newer slow cooker models feature a cast-aluminum insert that can be used on the stove top. If you have one of these, you can do the initial browning and deglazing in the insert, rather than in a frying pan or sauté pan as called for in the recipes. In most cases, you will still need to brown the item in batches to avoid crowding the insert.

SMALL SLOW COOKERS

In general, the recipes in this book will work well in a 5-quart (5-l) slow cooker. But if you are using a 3½- to 4-quart (3.5- to 4-l) slow cooker, you will need to cut the recipe by one-third or one-half. The cooking time will remain the same.

HEAT SETTINGS

Even though the recipes in some cookbooks suggest you can use the high heat setting instead of the low heat setting when you are in a hurry, and the dish will be ready in about half the time, it is not recommended for the recipes in this book. The higher heat setting on most slow cookers is 300°F (150°C), which will cause the liquid to simmer rapidly, rather than slowly, and can lead to tough protein, too much condensation, and less-than-stellar results. In most cases, the low setting of 200°F (95°C), used for the majority of the recipes in this book, is ideal for the slow-cooked alchemy that produces the best, most tender results.

Using Your Oven or Stove Top

The technique of slow cooking has a long history, which means that any recipe that works in the slow cooker can also be prepared as it was in the past, on the stove top or in the oven. Only minor adjustments to the ingredients, seasonings, and cooking times are necessary.

THE IDEAL VESSEL The recipes in this book were developed for long cooking in the consistent low temperature of a slow cooker, and neither the oven nor the stove top can match that steady, low heat. But the art of slow cooking long predates the invention of the slow cooker, which means that most of these recipes can be adapted to the oven or stove top.

The ideal vessel to use either in the oven or on the stove top is a Dutch oven, a large, heavy, round or oval pot with two loop handles and a tight-fitting lid. Cast iron ensures the best heat distribution, with enameled cast iron preferred for its resistance to sticking and because it will not react with wine, tomatoes, or other acidic ingredients that can give the dish an off flavor. You can brown directly in the Dutch oven, in batches as necessary, and then add other ingredients, liquids, and herbs and spices to the pot.

ADJUSTING LIQUIDS AND SEASONINGS As mentioned previously in The Basics (page 10), the quantities of liquids and seasonings in the recipes of this book are calibrated specifically for slow cookers. When converting recipes for the oven or stove top, use the following rough guidelines: double the amount of liquid and halve the amount of spices or dried herbs. Salt and pepper should remain the same. Check the amount of liquid during cooking, and add more if it seems too dry. Taste the dish during and after cooking, and adjust the seasonings to taste.

OVEN METHOD The even, circulating heat of the oven is particularly suited to braising larger cuts of meat, such as brisket, roasts, or shoulder. For the recipes in this book, preheat the oven to 325°F (165°C), place the filled Dutch oven on the center rack, and allow about 1 hour of oven time for every 3–3½ hours of slow-cooker time on the low setting. The dish is ready when the meat or other ingredients are tender when tested and the sauce is thickened as described in the recipe. Unlike when using a slow cooker, there is no need to put dense vegetables, such as potatoes and carrots, at the bottom of the Dutch oven (see Layering, page 10).

STOVE-TOP METHOD The variability of the heat is the main disadvantage to slow cooking on the stove top. The advantage, however, is that the cook has more control. Because soups and stews containing smaller pieces of meat or chicken parts and a relatively large quantity of liquid must be maintained at a constant simmer, they tend to fare better over a stove top burner. These dishes can also be more easily monitored on the stove top than in the oven.

You will need to adjust the heat every now and again, because as the liquid in the recipe reduces, it starts to boil more rapidly, which means the heat level must be lowered incrementally. Plan on about 1 hour at a gentle simmer on the stove top for every 3–3½ hours in the slow cooker on the low setting.

Adding Freshness

When foods are braised in a slow cooker, colors can fade, flavors can dull, and textures can soften. You can quickly and easily perk them up with a simple addition: a squeeze of citrus juice, a shower of chopped herbs, or a crunchy salad dressed with a lively vinaigrette.

The slow cooker has long been championed as the best way to cook deeply flavored, protein-packed braises and stews—the kind of hearty comfort food that nearly everyone craves now and again. To keep such dishes from becoming boring and too similar, every recipe in this book suggests a vivid color, a new flavor, a crunchy texture, and/or other elements that will add flair to the plate. The reason for these additions is simple: contemporary home cooks crave bright, fresh flavors and healthful ingredients, even when enjoying comfort food.

For example, braised short ribs are satisfying on their own, but if you add buttery avocado slices and a tangy tomatillo salsa, every bite tastes even better. Meaty slow-cooked lamb shanks are delicious, but topping them with pomegranate seeds and fresh mint sprigs makes them memorable. Even a simple addition can make a big difference. A squeeze of lime juice or a drizzle of vinegar added at the last minute will enhance the flavors in almost any dish, heightening them on the palate. Or, you might add flavor, color, and texture by finishing a dish with a scattering of fresh herbs—chopped basil, dill, parsley, or oregano— or a finely diced, crunchy vegetable, such as red bell pepper, jicama, fennel, or cucumber.

Salads are yet another way to add freshness to slow-cooked dishes. In the past, they were generally eaten before the main course and occasionally after.

Nowadays, salads appear as side dishes on menus almost as often as do cooked vegetables. Salads are especially welcome when they accompany hearty braised dishes, where their typically crisp texture and bright flavors nicely balances the richness that characterize slow cooking.

Spooning a tangle of fresh, crunchy vinaigrette-tossed ingredients on top of a braised meat, poultry, or fish dish is particularly appealing. The dressing mixes with the braising juices, so that each bite includes the flavors of both the braised dish and the salad. Ale-braised pork chops topped with a salad of peppery arugula and juicy peaches, and garlic-infused chicken thighs crowned with thinly sliced fennel dressed with a lemon vinaigrette are just two examples of salads delivering freshness.

Of course, this does not mean you should ignore more conventional sides. Slow-cooked meats and poultry almost always include a flavorful braising liquid, which means that they pair well with starchy dishes for enjoying the sauce. Creamy polenta, buttered egg noodles, fluffy mashed potatoes, steamed jasmine rice, or a loaf of crusty bread are popular choices. During the colder months, roasted vegetables, such as sweet potatoes, winter squashes, or turnips, are also good partners. And even if you are pressed for time, there are fast and easy options, including quick-cooking polenta or couscous or warm corn tortillas.

BEEF

Brisket, short ribs, flank steak, chuck—many of beef's leaner or tougher cuts become meltingly tender after a long, lazy stint in a slow cooker. When paired with a pantry full of distinctive ingredients—mangoes, chiles, daikon, corn, pineapple, tomatillos—these soulful braises deliver a complex mix of fresh, irresistible flavors to the table.

Asian-Style Short Ribs

6 lb (3 kg) beef short ribs, English cut, trimmed of most fat

Salt and freshly ground pepper

¾ teaspoon five-spice powder

¼ cup (2 oz/60 g) *each* hoisin sauce and ketchup, or ½ cup (4 oz/125 g) ketchup

2 tablespoons rice vinegar

2 tablespoons soy sauce

1 tablespoon Asian fish sauce

1 tablespoon honey

1 small yellow onion, finely chopped

1 tablespoon peeled and minced fresh ginger

5 cloves garlic, smashed

Daikon Salad for serving (see note; optional)

2 tablespoons chopped roasted peanuts or cashews (optional)

MAKES 6 SERVINGS

Preheat the broiler. Season the ribs all over with ¾ teaspoon each salt and pepper and the five-spice powder, and place on a rack set in a rimmed baking sheet. Broil, turning once, until nicely browned and sizzling on both sides, 8–10 minutes on each side.

In a slow cooker, stir together the hoisin sauce and ketchup, vinegar, soy sauce, fish sauce, honey, onion, ginger, and garlic. Add the ribs and turn to coat evenly with the hoisin mixture. Stack the thicker ribs at the bottom of the slow cooker. Cover and cook on the low setting for 6 hours. The meat should be very tender.

Remove the ribs from the slow cooker, and serve the meat on or off the bones. Divide among warm shallow bowls or plates, moisten each serving with some of the braising liquid, and top with a large spoonful of the salad, if using. Garnish with the nuts, if using, and serve at once.

ADD FRESHNESS WITH **DAIKON SALAD** In a bowl, combine 1 large daikon, about ¾ lb (375 g), peeled and julienned or shredded on the large holes of a box grater; 2 carrots, peeled and julienned or shredded on the large holes of a box grater; 1 shallot, minced; and ½ cup (½ oz/15 g) chopped fresh cilantro or flat-leaf parsley leaves. Add 3 tablespoons peanut oil and 1 tablespoon rice vinegar and toss to coat evenly.

Short Rib Tacos

3 dried ancho chiles

1½ tablespoons canola oil

1 yellow onion, finely chopped

1 green bell pepper, seeded and finely chopped

3 cloves garlic, finely chopped

½ cup (4 fl oz/125 ml) lager-style beer

1 tablespoon sherry vinegar

2 plum tomatoes, seeded and coarsely chopped

1½ teaspoons ground cumin

3 lb (1.5 kg) beef short ribs, English cut, trimmed of most fat

Salt and freshly ground pepper

½ teaspoon dried oregano

12 corn tortillas, each about 6 inches (15 cm) in diameter

Avocado-Tomatillo Salsa (see note) or purchased tomatillo salsa for serving

¼ cup (⅓ oz/10 g) coarsely chopped fresh cilantro leaves

MAKES 6 SERVINGS

Stem the chiles, slit lengthwise, and discard the seeds. Place in a heatproof bowl, cover with hot water, and let soak for 20–30 minutes to rehydrate. Drain and set the chiles aside.

Preheat the broiler. In a heavy frying pan over medium-high heat, warm the oil. Add the onion and bell pepper and sauté until softened and lightly golden, about 6 minutes. Add the garlic and cook for 1 minute more. Pour in the beer and vinegar and stir to dislodge any browned bits on the pan bottom. Transfer the contents of the pan to a blender, add the rehydrated chiles, tomatoes, and cumin, and process until smooth.

Season the short ribs all over with salt, pepper, and the oregano, and place on a rack set in a rimmed baking sheet. Broil, turning once, until nicely browned on all sides, 8–10 minutes on each side. Transfer the ribs to a slow cooker. Pour the chile mixture over the ribs, cover, and cook on the low setting for 8 hours. The meat should be very tender.

Remove the ribs. Pull the meat from the bones, shred the meat, and set aside. Pour the braising liquid into a saucepan and, using a large spoon, skim off the fat from the liquid. Place the pan over medium-high heat, bring to a brisk simmer, and simmer until reduced by about one-third, about 10 minutes. Add the shredded meat to the sauce.

Heat a nonstick frying pan or a griddle over medium heat. One at a time, warm the tortillas, turning once, for about 30 seconds on each side. Wrap in a kitchen towel to keep warm until all have been heated.

Using a slotted spoon, top the tortillas with the warm beef, dividing it evenly. Top each with some of the salsa and cilantro, and serve at once.

ADD ZING WITH **AVOCADO-TOMATILLO SALSA** In a blender or food processor, combine ½ lb (250 g) tomatillos, husks removed and quartered, and 1 or 2 jalapeño chiles, seeded and coarsely chopped. Process until chunky. Add ¼ cup (2 fl oz/60 ml) water; ½ small white onion, halved; ¼ cup (⅓ oz/10 g) fresh cilantro leaves and cut-up stems; and 1 teaspoon salt. Process until smooth. (At this point, the salsa can be refrigerated for up to 3 days.) Stir in 1 avocado, halved, pitted, peeled, and diced, before serving. Serve at room temperature or slightly chilled.

Smoky Beef Chili

4 lb (2 kg) boneless beef chuck, trimmed of most fat and cut into ¾-inch (2-cm) cubes

Salt and freshly ground pepper

¼ cup (2 fl oz/60 ml) canola oil

2 large yellow onions, coarsely chopped

8 cloves garlic, sliced

2 chipotle chiles in adobo sauce, finely chopped

2 tablespoons chipotle chile powder

2 teaspoons ground cumin

1 teaspoon dried oregano, preferably Mexican

½–1 teaspoon red pepper flakes

1 cup (8 oz/250 g) tomato paste

2–3 cups (16–24 fl oz/ 500–750 ml) beef stock, homemade (page 214) or purchased

Corn Salsa for serving (see note; optional)

MAKES 8 SERVINGS

Season the beef generously with salt and pepper. In a large, heavy frying pan over high heat, warm the oil. When the oil is hot, add half of the beef and sear, turning as needed to brown evenly, until golden brown on all sides, about 5 minutes total. Using a slotted spoon, transfer the beef to a plate. Repeat with the remaining beef and add to the plate.

Pour off most of the fat from the pan and return to medium heat. Add the onions and sauté until softened, about 6 minutes. Add the garlic and cook for 1 minute more. Add the chipotle chiles and sauce, chile powder, cumin, oregano, red pepper flakes to taste, and tomato paste, stir well, and cook for 2 minutes. Pour in 1 cup (8 fl oz/250 ml) of the stock and stir to dislodge any browned bits from the pan bottom. Transfer the contents of the pan to a slow cooker. Add 1 teaspoon salt, several grinds of pepper, and 1 cup stock if you prefer a thicker, more intensely flavored chili, or 2 cups (16 fl oz/500 ml) stock if you prefer a soupier chili (for spooning over rice or moistening corn bread). Stir in the browned beef. Cover and cook on the low setting for 5 hours. The meat should be very tender.

Ladle the chili into warm shallow bowls and top each serving with a heaping spoonful of the salsa, if using. Serve at once.

ADD FRESHNESS WITH CORN SALSA In a bowl, combine 2 cups (12 oz/375 g) fresh or thawed, frozen corn kernels; 2 cups (12 oz/375 g) grape or cherry tomatoes, halved; 4 green onions, including the light green tops, thinly sliced; and ⅓–½ cup (3–4 fl oz/80–125 ml) Lime Vinaigrette (page 216). Toss well.

Cuban-Style Stuffed Flank Steak

1½ lb (750 g) flank steak

¼ lb (125 g) smoked sausage such as andouille, finely chopped

½ cup (1 oz/30 g) fresh bread crumbs

1 large clove garlic, minced

2 tablespoons grated Parmesan cheese

2 tablespoons chopped fresh mint

½ teaspoon freshly grated nutmeg

Salt and freshly ground pepper

1 egg, lightly beaten

2 tablespoons olive oil

1 large yellow onion, finely chopped

2 carrots, peeled and finely chopped

1 teaspoon dried oregano

2 tablespoons tomato paste

½ cup (4 fl oz/125 ml) medium-dry sherry

1 can (15 oz/470 g) diced tomatoes, drained

3 bay leaves

Fresh Tomato Relish for serving (see note; optional)

MAKES 4–6 SERVINGS

Place the flank steak on a work surface and cover with a large sheet of plastic wrap. Using a meat pounder, pound it into a large rectangle about ¼ inch (6 mm) thick (or ask your butcher to do this).

In a bowl, mix together the sausage, bread crumbs, garlic, Parmesan, mint, and nutmeg and season with salt and pepper. Add the egg and mix well. Spread the sausage mixture evenly over the flank steak, leaving a ¼-inch border uncovered all around. Starting at one short end, roll up the steak into a spiral and tie securely with kitchen twine at 1½-inch (4-cm) intervals.

In a large, heavy frying pan over medium-high heat, warm the oil. When the oil is hot, add the rolled steak and cook, turning as needed with tongs, until well browned on all sides, about 10 minutes total. Transfer to a slow cooker. Add the onion, carrots, and oregano to the frying pan and sauté over medium-high heat until softened and beginning to brown, about 6 minutes. Stir in the tomato paste and cook for 1 minute more. Pour in the sherry and stir to dislodge any browned bits on the pan bottom. Stir in the tomatoes and bay leaves, and then transfer the contents of the pan to the slow cooker. Cover and cook on the low setting for 5 hours. The steak should be very tender.

Transfer the rolled steak to a cutting board, tent with aluminum foil, and let rest for 15 minutes. Remove and discard the bay leaves, but reserve the braising vegetables and liquid.

Snip the strings from the rolled steak and, using a sharp carving knife, cut crosswise into slices about ¾ inch (2 cm) thick. Spoon some of the braising liquid and vegetables over the slices, then top with the fresh tomato relish, if using. Serve at once.

ADD FLAVOR WITH **FRESH TOMATO RELISH** In a bowl, stir together 2 tomatoes, seeded and finely diced; ½ yellow bell pepper, seeded and finely diced; 3 green onions, including the light green tops, finely chopped; 1 tablespoon finely chopped red onion; 1 tablespoon *each* extra-virgin olive oil and sherry vinegar; and salt and pepper to taste.

Beef & Pumpkin Stew

3 lb (1.5 kg) beef bottom round, trimmed of most fat and cut into 1¼-inch (3-cm) chunks

Salt and freshly ground pepper

2 tablespoons olive oil

1 yellow onion, finely chopped

2 sprigs fresh thyme

3 bay leaves

4 cloves garlic, finely chopped

1 cinnamon stick

⅓ cup (3 fl oz/80 ml) dry red wine

2 tablespoons plus 1 teaspoon red wine vinegar

2 large carrots, peeled and cut into chunks

1 can (15 oz/470 g) diced tomatoes, drained

⅓ cup (3 fl oz/80 ml) beef or chicken stock, homemade (page 214) or purchased

1 lb (500 g) pumpkin or butternut squash, peeled, seeded, and cut into ¾-inch (2-cm) chunks

2 green onions, thinly sliced

1 tablespoon chopped fresh mint

MAKES 6 SERVINGS

Season the beef generously with salt and pepper. In a large, heavy frying pan over medium-high heat, warm 1 tablespoon of the olive oil. When it is hot, working in batches to avoid crowding, add the beef and sauté until golden brown on all sides, about 8 minutes total. Using a slotted spoon, transfer the beef to a plate.

Pour off most of the fat from the pan and return to medium-high heat. Add the onion, thyme sprigs, and bay leaves and sauté until the onion begins to brown, about 6 minutes. Add the garlic and cinnamon and cook for 1 minute more. Pour in the wine and the 2 tablespoons vinegar and stir to dislodge any browned bits on the pan bottom. Transfer the contents of the pan to a slow cooker and stir in the carrots, tomatoes, and stock. Add the beef, cover, and cook on the low setting for 5 hours.

Scatter the pumpkin over the top of the beef, re-cover, and continue to cook for 3 hours more. The beef and pumpkin should be very tender.

Remove and discard the thyme sprigs, cinnamon stick, and bay leaves. Let the stew stand for 5 minutes, then, using a large spoon, skim off the fat.

In a small bowl, whisk together the remaining 1 tablespoon olive oil and 1 teaspoon vinegar, ¼ teaspoon salt, and several grinds of pepper. Stir in the green onions and mint.

Divide the stew evenly among warm bowls and spoon the green onion mixture over top. Serve at once.

In this flavorful and healthful take on a traditional autumn dish, the addition of a light vinaigrette laced with green onions and peppery mint just before serving infuses the stew with bright, fresh flavors. Serve this hearty stew over steamed couscous.

Classic Beef Stew

3 lb (1.5 kg) beef bottom round, trimmed of most fat and cut into 2-inch (5-cm) chunks

Salt and freshly ground pepper

¾ cup (4 oz/125 g) flour

2 tablespoons canola oil

4 cloves garlic, smashed

1½ cups (12 fl oz/375 ml) dry red wine such as Pinot Noir or Zinfandel

1 cup (8 fl oz/250 ml) beef or chicken stock, homemade (page 214) or purchased

3 sprigs fresh thyme

3 bay leaves

3 large carrots, peeled, halved lengthwise, and cut into chunks

½ lb (250 g) cremini mushrooms, brushed clean and quartered

1 bag (10 oz/315 g) frozen pearl onions, thawed and drained

Frisée and Bacon Salad for serving (see note; optional)

MAKES 6 SERVINGS

Season the beef generously with salt and pepper, then place in a plastic bag with the flour and shake the bag to coat the beef evenly. Remove from the bag and tap off the excess flour. In a large, heavy frying pan over medium-high heat, warm the oil. When the oil is hot, working in batches if necessary to avoid crowding, add the beef and sear, turning as needed, until golden on all sides, 8–10 minutes total. Transfer to a slow cooker.

Pour off most of the fat from the frying pan and return to medium-high heat. Add the garlic and cook for about 1 minute. Pour in the wine and stir to dislodge any browned bits on the pan bottom. Add the stock, thyme sprigs, and bay leaves and pour the contents of the pan over the beef. Stir in the carrots, cover, and cook on the low setting for 6 hours.

Stir in the mushrooms and pearl onions, re-cover, and cook for 1 hour more. The meat and vegetables should be very tender.

Remove and discard the bay leaves and thyme, let the stew stand for a few minutes, and then skim the fat from the top with a large spoon.

Ladle the stew into warm shallow bowls, top each serving with some of the salad, if using, and serve at once.

ADD CRUNCH WITH **FRISÉE AND BACON SALAD** Cut 6 oz (185 g) thick-cut bacon slices crosswise into strips ¼ inch (6 mm) wide. In a frying pan over medium heat, fry the bacon until crisp and golden, 3–5 minutes. Using a slotted spoon, transfer to paper towels to drain. Place 1 head frisée, torn into bite-size pieces, into a bowl with the bacon, drizzle with ⅓–½ cup (3–4 fl oz/80–125 ml) Shallot Vinaigrette (page 216), and toss to coat evenly.

Thai-Style Brisket

2-lb (1-kg) beef brisket, trimmed of most fat

Salt and freshly ground pepper

2 tablespoons olive oil

1 large yellow onion, coarsely chopped

1 carrot, peeled and coarsely chopped

5 cloves garlic, smashed

1 stalk lemongrass, bulb portion only, tough outer leaves removed and thinly sliced (optional)

¼ cup (2 fl oz/60 ml) dry white wine

½ cup (4 fl oz/125 ml) chicken or beef stock, homemade (page 214) or purchased

¼ cup (2 fl oz/60 ml) soy sauce

Pineapple Relish for serving (see note)

MAKES 6 SERVINGS

Season the brisket generously all over with salt and pepper. In a large frying pan over medium-high heat, warm the oil. When the oil is hot, add the brisket and sear, turning as needed, until deep golden brown on all sides, about 10 minutes total. Transfer the brisket to a plate.

Pour off most of the fat from the pan and return to medium-high heat. Add the onion and carrot and sauté until softened and lightly colored, about 6 minutes. Add the garlic and lemongrass and cook for 1 minute more. Pour in the wine and stir to dislodge any browned bits on the pan bottom. Stir in the stock, soy sauce, and several grinds of pepper. Transfer the contents of the pan to a slow cooker and place the brisket and any accumulated juices on top. Cover and cook on the low setting for about 8 hours, turning the brisket over halfway through if possible. The brisket should be very tender.

Transfer the brisket to a cutting board and let rest for a few minutes. The braising liquid can be served with the brisket; if using, skim the fat from the surface with a large spoon. Cut the brisket across the grain into slices.

Divide the brisket slices among warm individual plates. If desired, spoon some of the braising liquid around each serving, then spoon the relish over the slices. Serve at once.

ADD FRESHNESS WITH **PINEAPPLE RELISH** In a bowl, toss together 1 cup (8 oz/250 g) finely diced fresh or canned pineapple; 2 tablespoons finely diced red bell pepper; 1 tablespoon minced red onion; 1 teaspoon Thai sweet chile sauce; 1½ teaspoons Asian fish sauce; 2 teaspoons soy sauce; 1 teaspoon minced fresh cilantro; and 6 fresh mint leaves, minced. Use right away, or cover and refrigerate for up to 4 hours before serving.

Picadillo Tostadas

1½ lb (750 g) boneless beef chuck, trimmed of most fat and cut into ½-inch (12-mm) cubes

Salt and freshly ground pepper

2 tablespoons canola oil, plus more for frying

1 yellow onion, finely chopped

3 cloves garlic, finely chopped

2 small Granny Smith or other tart green apples, peeled, cored, and coarsely grated

1 cup (6 oz/185 g) canned crushed tomatoes

2 tablespoons cider vinegar

3 bay leaves

1 teaspoon ground cumin

¼ teaspoon ground cinnamon

⅛ teaspoon ground cloves

⅓ cup (2 oz/60 g) golden raisins

½ cup (2½ oz/75 g) toasted almond slivers, chopped

6 corn tortillas, each about 6 inches (15 cm) in diameter

Veggie Slaw (see note) or shredded cabbage for serving

2–3 tablespoons coarsely chopped fresh cilantro

MAKES 6 SERVINGS

Season the beef generously all over with salt and pepper. In a large, heavy frying pan over medium-high heat, warm the 2 tablespoons oil. When the oil is hot, working in batches if necessary to avoid crowding, add the beef and sauté until browned on all sides, 6–8 minutes total. Using a slotted spoon, transfer the beef to a slow cooker.

Pour off most of the fat from the pan and return to medium heat. Add the onion and sauté until softened, about 5 minutes. Add the garlic and sauté for 1 minute more. Transfer the contents of the pan to the slow cooker and stir in the apples, tomatoes, vinegar, bay leaves, cumin, cinnamon, cloves, raisins, ½ teaspoon salt, and several grinds of pepper. Cover and cook on the low setting for 5 hours, stirring halfway through if possible. The meat should be very tender.

Using a slotted spoon, transfer the meat and vegetables to a serving bowl. Remove and discard the bay leaves. Using a large spoon, skim the fat from the braising liquid. Add just enough of the liquid to the meat to make it juicy, and discard the remainder. Fold in the almonds and keep warm.

Pour oil to a depth of 1 inch (2.5 cm) into a small frying pan. Over medium-high heat, warm the oil until hot but not smoking. One at a time, add the tortillas and fry, turning once with tongs, until crisp and golden, about 30 seconds for each side. Transfer to paper towels to drain.

Place a fried tortilla on each plate and top each with an equal amount of the beef picadillo. Top each with a generous spoonful of the slaw, sprinkle with the cilantro, and serve at once.

ADD CRUNCH WITH **VEGGIE SLAW** In a large bowl, combine 1 cup (3 oz/90 g) *each* coarsely shredded green cabbage and red cabbage; ½ cup (1½ oz/45 g) shredded carrot; 1 small red bell pepper, seeded and cut into matchsticks (optional); ½ teaspoon salt; ¼–½ teaspoon sugar, to taste; and several grinds of pepper. Drizzle in 3 tablespoons extra-virgin olive oil and toss to mix. Drizzle in 2 tablespoons cider vinegar and toss again.

Mediterranean Osso Buco with Orzo

3 lb (1.5 kg) veal shanks, cut crosswise into pieces about 1½ inches (4 cm) wide

Salt and freshly ground pepper

2 tablespoons olive oil

1 yellow onion, finely chopped

1 large carrot, peeled and finely chopped

2 stalks celery, finely chopped

4 cloves garlic, finely chopped

3 bay leaves

½ cup (4 fl oz/125 ml) dry white wine

½ cup (4 fl oz/125 ml) chicken stock, homemade (page 214) or purchased

1 can (15 oz/470 g) diced tomatoes, drained

1 lb (500 g) dried orzo

1½ tablespoons finely chopped fresh mint

Seeds of 1 pomegranate (optional)

⅓–½ cup (3–4 fl oz/80–125 ml) Shallot Vinaigrette (page 216)

MAKES 6 SERVINGS

Season the veal shanks generously all over with salt and pepper. In a large, heavy frying pan over medium-high heat, warm the oil. When the oil is hot, working in batches if necessary to avoid crowding, add the veal shanks and brown, turning once, until browned on all sides, 7–8 minutes total. Transfer the shanks to a plate.

Pour off most of the fat from the pan and return to medium-high heat. Add the onion, carrot, and celery and sauté until lightly golden, about 6 minutes. Add the garlic and bay leaves and cook for 1 minute more. Pour in the wine and stock and stir to dislodge any browned bits on the pan bottom. Transfer the contents of the pan to a slow cooker, and stir in the tomatoes. Place the veal shanks and any accumulated juices on top. Cover and cook on the low setting for 6 hours. The veal should be tender.

Transfer the veal to a plate and keep warm. Remove and discard the bay leaves from the slow cooker, and transfer the contents to a saucepan. Let stand for a few minutes, then use a large spoon to skim the fat from the top. Place over medium-high heat, bring to a rapid simmer, and cook until slightly reduced and thickened, about 5 minutes.

Meanwhile, bring a large pot three-fourths full of salted water to a boil, add the orzo, stir well, and cook until al dente, according to package directions. Drain and transfer to a large bowl. Add the mint, two-thirds of the pomegranate seeds (if using), and the vinaigrette and toss well.

Divide the orzo among warm individual plates and arrange the veal shanks on top. Garnish with the remaining pomegranate seeds (if using), and top with some of the reduced braising liquid. Serve at once.

Here, the rich braising juices that develop in the slow cooker mix with the bright flavors of the vinaigrette used to dress the orzo, creating a delectable result. A garnish of tart-sweet pomegranate seeds delivers a bold flavor and crunchy texture. If pomegranate seeds are unavailable, you can substitute dried cherries or cranberries, though the flavor will be sweeter.

Corned Beef with Cabbage

1 large yellow onion, coarsely chopped

1 large carrot, peeled and coarsely chopped

1 stalk celery, coarsely chopped

3 bay leaves

2 whole cloves

1 cup (8 fl oz/250 ml) apple juice, preferably unfiltered

1 corned beef brisket, 4–5 lb (2–2.5 kg), trimmed of most fat

1 small head green cabbage, about 2 lb (1 kg)

½ red onion, finely chopped

1 teaspoon caraway seeds

½ cup (4 fl oz/125 ml) olive oil

Salt and freshly ground pepper

2 tablespoons whole-grain mustard

3 tablespoons sherry vinegar

½ red bell pepper, seeded and finely chopped

2 tablespoons finely chopped fresh flat-leaf parsley

MAKES 6 SERVINGS

In a slow cooker, combine the onion, carrot, celery, bay leaves, and cloves. Add 1 cup (8 fl oz/250 ml) water and the apple juice, stir well, and place the brisket on top of the vegetables. Cover and cook on the low setting for 8 hours, turning the brisket halfway through if possible. The meat should be very tender.

Meanwhile, halve, core, and thinly slice the cabbage and place in a large, heatproof bowl. In a small saucepan over medium heat, combine the red onion, caraway seeds, olive oil, and several grinds of pepper, and bring to a gentle simmer. Cook until the onion is tender, 12–15 minutes. Remove from the heat, stir in the whole-grain mustard (don't worry if the mixture is lumpy), and pour over the cabbage. Immediately toss the cabbage with tongs until it wilts and is glossy. Season with ½ teaspoon salt, a little more pepper, and the sherry vinegar. Taste and adjust the seasoning. Add the bell pepper and parsley and mix well.

Transfer the brisket to a cutting board and let rest for a few minutes. Discard all but ½ cup (4 fl oz/125 ml) of the braising liquid and all of the vegetables (which will be mushy).

Slice the brisket across the grain, arrange the slices on a platter, and drizzle with the reserved braising liquid. Spoon the cabbage salad over or alongside the brisket slices. Serve at once.

The sparkling flavors of both mustard and sherry vinegar in the warm cabbage salad mingle with the succulent juices of the corned beef, to create an appealingly fresh dish. Simply steamed tiny red potatoes are a nice addition to round out the meal.

Braised Beef with Arugula & Grapefruit Salad

1 beef bottom round, about 3½ lb (1.75 kg), trimmed of most fat and tied

Salt and freshly ground pepper

2 tablespoons olive oil

1 yellow onion, sliced

1 stalk celery, sliced

½ cup (4 fl oz/125 ml) apple juice, preferably unfiltered

3 bay leaves

Arugula and Grapefruit Salad for serving (see note)

MAKES 6 SERVINGS

Season the beef generously all over with salt and pepper. In a large frying pan over medium-high heat, warm the oil. When the oil is hot, add the beef and sear, turning as needed, until deep golden brown on all sides, about 10 minutes total. Transfer the beef to a plate.

Pour off most of the fat from the pan and return to medium-high heat. Add the onion and celery and sauté until golden, about 6 minutes. Pour in the apple juice and stir to dislodge any browned bits on the pan bottom. Transfer the contents of the pan to a slow cooker, add the bay leaves, and place the beef on top. Cover and cook on the low setting for 8 hours. The beef should be very tender.

Transfer the beef to a cutting board and let rest for about 5 minutes. Meanwhile, using a large spoon, skim the fat from the braising liquid. Snip the strings on the beef and shred with 2 forks or slice across the grain.

Divide the beef among individual plates, and spoon enough of the braising liquid on top to moisten (reserve the remainder for another use or discard). Mound the salad on top of or alongside the beef. Serve at once.

ADD FRESHNESS WITH **ARUGULA AND GRAPEFRUIT SALAD** In a bowl, whisk together 1½ tablespoons white wine vinegar, 1 teaspoon honey mustard, ¼ teaspoon salt, and a few grinds of pepper. Whisk in ¼ cup (2 fl oz/60 ml) extra-virgin olive oil. Add 4 cups (4 oz/125 g) baby arugula; 2 avocados, halved, pitted, peeled, and sliced lengthwise ½ inch (12 mm) thick; 1 large grapefruit, peeled and segmented (page 217); ⅔ cup (3 oz/90 g) hazelnuts, toasted and skinned (page 217); and 4 large fresh basil leaves, finely slivered (optional). Toss gently to mix.

Beef with Endive & Sun-Dried Tomatoes

3 lb (1.5 kg) beef bottom round, trimmed of most fat and cut into large chunks

Salt and freshly ground pepper

5 tablespoons (3 fl oz/80 ml) olive oil

6 cloves garlic, smashed

1⅓ cups (11 fl oz/345 ml) beef stock, homemade (page 214) or purchased

¼ cup (2 fl oz/60 ml) white wine

3 sprigs fresh thyme

3 bay leaves

2 teaspoons Dijon mustard

2 tablespoons sherry vinegar

2 tablespoons walnut oil

2 large heads Belgian endive, cored and coarsely chopped

½ cup (2½ oz/75 g) green olives, pitted and chopped

½ cup (4 oz/125 g) oil-packed sun-dried tomatoes, sliced

Grated zest of 1 lemon

2 tablespoons chopped fresh flat-leaf parsley

MAKES 4–6 SERVINGS

Season the beef generously all over with salt and pepper. In a large, heavy frying pan over medium-high heat, warm 2 tablespoons of the olive oil. When the oil is hot, working in batches if necessary to avoid crowding, add the beef and sear, turning as needed, until browned on all sides, about 8 minutes total. Using a slotted spoon, transfer the beef to a slow cooker.

Pour off most of the fat from the pan and return to medium-high heat. Add the garlic and cook for 1 minute. Pour in the stock and wine and stir to dislodge any browned bits on the pan bottom. Add the thyme sprigs and bay leaves and transfer the contents of the pan to the slow cooker. Cover and cook on the low setting for 5–6 hours. The beef should be tender but still moist.

Just before the beef is ready, in a bowl, whisk together the mustard, vinegar, walnut oil, the remaining 3 tablespoons olive oil, ¼ teaspoon salt, and a few grinds of pepper. Add the endive, olives, sun-dried tomatoes, lemon zest, and parsley and toss to mix.

Using a slotted spoon, transfer the beef to a cutting board and shred with 2 forks. Transfer to warm individual plates or a platter. Moisten the beef with some of the braising liquid, if desired. Mound the endive salad on top of or alongside the beef. Serve at once.

This dish is perfect for wintertime when you crave robust flavors but want a relatively light main course—one that will satisfy both salad eaters and meat eaters alike. The mixture of endive, sun-dried tomatoes, and olives imparts a pleasantly sharp note to the slow-braised beef. Accompany with boiled small potatoes tossed with butter and parsley.

Braised Brisket with Chimichurri

2-lb (1-kg) beef brisket, trimmed of most fat

Salt and freshly ground pepper

2 tablespoons olive oil

1 large yellow onion, coarsely chopped

1 carrot, peeled and coarsely chopped

5 cloves garlic, smashed

1 teaspoon dried oregano

½ cup (4 fl oz/125 ml) dry red wine

½ cup (4 fl oz/125 ml) chicken or beef stock, homemade (page 214) or purchased

Chimichurri Sauce for serving (see note)

2 cups (12 oz/375 g) small cherry or grape tomatoes, halved, for serving

MAKES 6 SERVINGS

Season the brisket generously on all sides with salt and pepper. In a large, heavy frying pan over medium-high heat, warm the oil. When it is hot, add the brisket, and sear, turning once, until deep golden brown on both sides, about 5 minutes on each side. Transfer the brisket to a plate.

Pour off most of the fat from the pan and return to medium-high heat. Add the onion and carrot and sauté until softened and lightly colored, about 5 minutes. Add the garlic and oregano and cook for about 1 minute more. Pour in the wine and stir to dislodge any browned bits from the pan bottom. Stir in 1 teaspoon salt, several grinds of pepper, and the stock. Transfer the contents of the pan to a slow cooker and place the brisket and any accumulated juices on top. Cover and cook on the low setting for 9 hours, turning the brisket over halfway through if possible. The brisket should be very tender.

Transfer the brisket to a cutting board and let rest for a few minutes. Meanwhile, using a large spoon, skim the fat from the braising liquid. Cut the brisket crosswise against the grain into thick slices.

Arrange the brisket slices on a warm platter or individual plates and spoon some of the braising liquid around the sides. Drizzle with the chimichurri sauce and sprinkle with the cherry tomatoes. Serve at once.

ADD FRESHNESS WITH **CHIMICHURRI SAUCE** In a food processor, combine 1½ cups (1½ oz/45 g) firmly packed flat-leaf parsley leaves and cut-up tender stems; 6 cloves garlic, quartered; and 2 tablespoons fresh oregano leaves. Process until finely chopped. (Alternatively, finely chop the ingredients by hand.) Stir in ¾ cup (6 fl oz/180 ml) extra-virgin olive oil, 2 teaspoons coarse sea salt, 1 teaspoon freshly ground pepper, and ¼ teaspoon red pepper flakes (optional). Use at once, or cover and refrigerate for up to 4 hours. Just before serving, stir in 3 tablespoons white wine vinegar.

Short Rib Ragù

3 lb (1.5 kg) beef short ribs, English cut, trimmed of most fat

Salt and freshly ground pepper

2 tablespoons olive oil

2 slices thick-cut bacon, finely chopped

1 yellow onion, finely chopped

1 large carrot, peeled and finely chopped

2 stalks celery, finely chopped

10 cloves garlic, chopped

2 tablespoons tomato paste

¾ cup (6 fl oz/180 ml) red wine

1 can (28 oz/875 g) plum tomatoes, drained

2 sprigs fresh thyme

2 sprigs fresh rosemary

2 teaspoons red wine vinegar

1 lb (500 kg) dried pappardelle

½ cup (2 oz/60 g) grated Parmesan cheese

¼ cup (⅓ oz/10 g) *each* chopped fresh basil and fresh flat-leaf parsley

MAKES 6 SERVINGS

Pat the ribs dry and season with salt and pepper. In a large frying pan over medium-high heat, warm the oil. When the oil is hot, working in batches to avoid crowding, add the ribs and sear, turning as needed, until browned on all sides, 10–12 minutes. Using tongs, transfer the ribs to a slow cooker.

Pour off the fat from the pan and return it to medium heat. Add the bacon and cook, stirring, until the fat begins to render, about 2 minutes. Add the onion, carrot, and celery and cook, stirring occasionally, until golden, about 10 minutes. Add the garlic and tomato paste and stir for 2 minutes. Pour in the wine and stir to dislodge any browned bits on the pan bottom. Add the tomatoes, thyme, rosemary, vinegar, ¾ teaspoon salt, and several grinds of pepper, stir well, and bring the mixture to a simmer. Transfer the contents of the pan to the slow cooker, spooning it over the ribs. Cover and cook on the low setting for 8 hours. The ribs should be very tender.

Using the tongs, transfer the ribs to a platter and let cool slightly. Pull the meat from the bones, shred the meat, and set aside. Discard the herb sprigs. Using a large spoon, skim away the fat from the braising liquid. Transfer about three-fourths of the braising liquid to a blender or food processor and process to a smooth purée. Return the purée to the slow cooker and stir in the meat. Cover and keep warm.

Bring a large pot three-fourths full of salted water to a boil, add the pappardelle, stir well, and cook until al dente, according to package directions. Drain the pasta. Add the pasta to the slow cooker along with half of the cheese and toss to coat evenly. Divide among warm shallow bowls and garnish with the basil and parsley. Serve at once. Pass the remaining cheese at the table.

During fall and winter, this hearty pasta dish, fragrant with herbs, is a welcome centerpiece on the supper table. Round out the menu with a green salad and a loaf of crusty bread. To make removing the fat from the sauce easier, pour the sauce into a clear glass pitcher, let it settle for a few minutes, then skim off the fat with a large spoon.

Spicy Brisket & Tomato Panini

2-lb (1-kg) beef brisket, trimmed of most fat

Salt and freshly ground pepper

2 tablespoons olive oil, plus more for brushing

1 yellow onion, cut into large chunks

1 carrot, peeled and cut into large chunks

4 cloves garlic, smashed

1 teaspoon dried oregano

½ cup (4 fl oz/125 ml) dry red wine

½ cup (4 fl oz/125 ml) beef or chicken stock, homemade (page 214) or purchased

12 slices coarse country bread

Horseradish Mayonnaise (page 215)

2 large tomatoes such as beefsteak, cut into 12 slices

MAKES 6 SERVINGS

Season the brisket generously on all sides with salt and pepper. In a large, heavy frying pan over medium-high heat, warm the oil. When the oil is hot, add the brisket, and sear, turning once, until deep golden brown on both sides, about 5 minutes on each side. Transfer the brisket to a plate.

Pour off most of the fat from the pan and return it to medium-high heat. Add the onion and carrot and sauté until softened and lightly golden, about 5 minutes. Add the garlic and oregano and cook for 1 minute more. Pour in the wine and stir to dislodge any browned bits on the pan bottom. Stir in 1 teaspoon salt, several grinds of pepper, and the stock. Transfer the contents of the pan to a slow cooker, and place the brisket and any accumulated juices on top. Cover and cook on the low setting for about 8 hours, turning the brisket over halfway through if possible. The meat should be very tender. Transfer the brisket to a platter. Let cool slightly, then using 2 forks, shred the meat. If desired, strain the braising liquid, skim away the fat, and reserve the braising liquid for another use.

Preheat an electric panini grill or a heavy sauté pan over medium heat. Lightly brush 1 side of each bread slice with oil and place oiled side down on a work surface. Spread each bread slice with the mayonnaise. Place 2 tomato slices on 6 of the bread slices, and mound the shredded beef in an even layer over the tomatoes. Top with the remaining bread slices, mayonnaise side down. Working in batches, place the sandwiches in the grill and close the top plate, or place in the sauté pan and press down firmly with a flat, heavy pot lid. Cook the sandwiches (if using a sauté pan, turn once at the halfway point and press occasionally with the pot lid) until the bread is golden, about 5 minutes. Cut in half and serve at once.

For this satisfying weekend lunch or casual weeknight supper, freshly sliced tomato and spicy horseradish-laced mayonnaise are paired with tender beef brisket in crisp panini sandwiches. Accompany the sandwiches with a cup of hot soup or a tangle of vinaigrette-dressed salad greens. Strain and defat the flavorful braising liquid for use in another soup, stew, or braise.

Beef Adobo

5 lb (2.5 kg) beef shanks, cut crosswise into pieces about ½ inch (12 mm) wide

Salt and freshly ground pepper

2 tablespoons peanut oil

1 yellow onion, finely chopped

1 large carrot, peeled and finely chopped

10 cloves garlic, smashed

3 bay leaves

4 whole star anise

1 cup (8 fl oz/250 ml) rice vinegar

½ cup (4 fl oz/125 ml) soy sauce, preferably low sodium

2 hearts of romaine lettuce, leaves separated

Mango Salsa for serving, homemade (see note) or purchased

MAKES 4–6 SERVINGS

Season the shanks lightly all over with salt and pepper. In a large, heavy frying pan over medium-high heat, warm the oil. When the oil is hot, working in batches if necessary to avoid crowding, add the shanks and sear, turning as needed, until browned on both sides, about 8 minutes total. Transfer the shanks to a slow cooker and spread in an even layer.

Pour off most of the fat from the pan and return it to medium-high heat. Add the onion and carrot and sauté until softened and just beginning to brown, about 6 minutes. Add the garlic, bay leaves, and star anise and cook for 1 minute more. Pour in the vinegar and soy sauce and stir to dislodge any browned bits on the pan bottom. Transfer the contents of the pan to the slow cooker. Cover and cook on the low setting for 8 hours, basting the meat with the braising liquid two or three times if possible. The beef should be very tender.

Transfer the beef shanks to a plate and keep warm. Strain the braising liquid into a small saucepan, and retrieve the garlic cloves from the sieve. Let the liquid stand for a few minutes, and then skim away the fat with a large spoon. Using a fork, smash the garlic cloves into a paste, then add to the braising liquid. Bring to a rapid simmer over high heat and cook until slightly reduced, about 5 minutes.

Meanwhile, remove the meat from the bones and discard the bones. Shred the meat with 2 forks. Moisten the meat with the reduced braising liquid.

Arrange the lettuce leaves on a platter or individual plates, spoon the meat over or alongside the leaves, top with the salsa, and serve at once.

ADD FLAVOR WITH **MANGO SALSA** In a bowl, combine 2 mangoes, peeled, pitted, and diced (about 2 cups/12 oz/ 375 g); 1 small red bell pepper, seeded and diced; 1 small serrano chile, seeded and minced; 4 green onions, including the light green tops, thinly sliced; ¼ cup (⅓ oz/10 g) coarsely chopped fresh cilantro; 1½ tablespoons fresh lime juice; and ¼–½ teaspoon salt. Toss together gently, and then cover and refrigerate for at least 30 minutes or up to 1 hour.

Shredded Brisket & Chutney Sandwiches

1 can (15 oz/470 g) diced tomatoes, including juice

2/3 cup (5 fl oz/160 ml) beef or chicken stock, homemade (page 214) or purchased

1/3 cup (3 fl oz/80 ml) dry red or white wine

1 yellow onion, cut into large chunks

4 whole cloves garlic

1 teaspoon dried oregano

Salt and freshly ground pepper

2-lb (1-kg) beef brisket, trimmed of most fat

6 pieces focaccia, each about 5 inches (13 cm) square

Plum Chutney (see note) or purchased fruit chutney

4 cups (4 oz/125 g) loosely packed watercress or arugula, tough stems removed

MAKES 6 SERVINGS

In a slow cooker, combine the tomatoes, stock, wine, onion, garlic, oregano, 1 teaspoon salt, and several grinds of pepper. Stir well, and then top with the brisket. Cover and cook on the low setting for 8 hours, turning the brisket over halfway through if possible. The brisket should be very tender.

Transfer the brisket to a platter and let rest for a few minutes. Then, using 2 forks, shred the meat. Strain the braising liquid, skim away the fat, and drizzle just enough liquid over the shredded meat to moisten it. Reserve the remaining liquid for another use or discard.

Split each focaccia square horizontally. Spread a thick layer of chutney on each focaccia bottom. Top each sandwich with some of the shredded brisket and the watercress, and close with the focaccia tops, pressing down gently. Cut each sandwich in half on the diagonal and serve.

ADD ZING WITH **PLUM CHUTNEY** In a saucepan over medium heat, combine 1 shallot, finely chopped; 1 tablespoon peeled and finely chopped fresh ginger; 3 tablespoons white wine vinegar; 1½ tablespoons firmly packed dark brown sugar; ¼ teaspoon salt; and ⅛ teaspoon red pepper flakes. Bring to a simmer, stirring constantly. Cover and cook until the shallot has softened, about 5 minutes. Stir in 3 large plums, pitted and cut into ¾-inch (2-cm) chunks; re-cover partially and cook until the mixture is jamlike, 10–15 minutes. Let cool before using.

PORK & LAMB

Mild-flavored pork and lamb share an affinity for pungent garlic, earthy rosemary, tangy citrus, sweet peppers, fruity olive oil, and more. Nearly every cut of these versatile meats, from lean chops to marbled shoulder roasts, meaty shanks to chewy ribs, can be left to braise leisurely in a slow cooker, emerging melt-in-your-mouth tender and succulent at suppertime.

Orange-Braised Pork Chops

6 bone-in pork loin chops, each about 1½ inches (4 cm) thick

Salt and freshly ground pepper

2 tablespoons olive oil

2 large shallots, halved and thinly sliced

4 cloves garlic, sliced

½ cup (4 fl oz/125 ml) dry white wine

½ cup (4 fl oz/125 ml) chicken stock, homemade (page 214) or purchased

2 tablespoons white wine vinegar

Finely grated zest of 2 oranges (reserve oranges if making salad; see note)

Spinach and Orange Salad for serving (see note; optional)

MAKES 6 SERVINGS

Season the pork chops generously on both sides with salt and pepper. In a large, heavy frying pan over medium-high heat, warm the oil. When the oil is hot, working in batches if necessary to avoid crowding, add the chops and sear, turning once, until golden brown on both sides, 8–10 minutes total. Transfer the chops to a plate.

Pour off most of the fat from the pan and return it to medium-high heat. Add the shallots and garlic and sauté until they begin to brown, about 6 minutes. Pour in the wine and stir to dislodge any browned bits from the pan bottom. Stir in the stock, vinegar, orange zest, ½ teaspoon salt, and several grinds of pepper. Transfer the contents of the pan to a slow cooker and stack the pork chops on top. Cover and cook on the low setting for 7 hours. The chops should be tender.

Divide the pork chops among warm individual plates. Spoon the braising liquid over the chops, top with the salad, if using, and serve.

ADD FRESHNESS WITH **SPINACH AND ORANGE SALAD** Trim the remaining peel and pith from the 2 oranges and segment them as directed on page 217. Roughly chop the orange segments. In a bowl, whisk together 1½ tablespoons white wine vinegar, 1 teaspoon Dijon mustard, ¼ teaspoon salt, and several grinds of pepper. Whisk in ¼ cup (2 fl oz/ 60 ml) extra-virgin olive oil. Add 5–6 cups (5–6 oz/155–185 g) baby spinach, the orange segments, and 2 tablespoons finely snipped fresh chives (optional) and toss to mix.

Pork with Spicy Squash

3-lb (1.5-kg) boneless pork shoulder, trimmed of visible fat

Salt and freshly ground pepper

2 tablespoons peanut oil

1 large yellow onion, finely chopped

4 cloves garlic, smashed

2 tablespoons dry sake, dry white wine, or white vermouth

½ cup (4 fl oz/125 ml) chicken stock, homemade (page 214) or purchased

1-lb (500-g) butternut squash, peeled and cut into 1-inch (2.5-cm) cubes

1 tablespoon olive oil

¼ cup (⅓ oz/10 g) chopped fresh Thai or sweet basil

¼ cup (⅓ oz/10 g) coarsely chopped fresh cilantro

⅓–½ cup (3–4 fl oz/ 80–125 ml) Asian Lime Vinaigrette (page 216)

1 or 2 small red serrano chiles, seeded and thinly sliced

MAKES 6 SERVINGS

Season the pork generously all over with salt and pepper. In a large frying pan over medium-high heat, warm the peanut oil. When the oil is hot, add the pork and sear, turning as needed, until golden brown on all sides, about 10 minutes total. Transfer the pork to a slow cooker.

Pour off some of the fat from the frying pan and return it to medium-high heat. Add the onion and sauté until softened and lightly golden, about 7 minutes. Add the garlic and cook for 1 minute more. Pour in the sake and stir to dislodge any browned bits on the pan bottom. Stir in the stock and pour the contents of the pan over the pork. Cover and cook on the low setting for 8 hours. The pork should be very tender.

About 30 minutes before the pork has finished cooking, preheat the oven to 450°F (230°C). In a small roasting pan, toss together the squash and olive oil. Season generously with salt and pepper. Roast, stirring every 5 minutes, until tender, about 15 minutes. Let cool for 5–10 minutes, then transfer to a bowl. Add the basil, cilantro, and the vinaigrette and chiles to taste and toss to coat evenly.

Transfer the pork to a cutting board and let cool slightly. Meanwhile, using a large spoon, skim the fat from the braising liquid. Cut the pork into slices across the grain, then shred with 2 forks. Spoon a little of the braising liquid onto the meat to moisten.

Divide the pork and roasted squash among warm individual plates or mound onto a serving platter and serve at once.

This colorful dish dresses up winter squash with bright Asian flavors and combines it with tender shredded pork to make a light yet filling supper. Pork shoulder is well marbled, which makes it particularly flavorful. If you prefer to use leaner pork loin for this dish, reduce the braising time to 6 hours, and moisten the meat with plenty of braising liquid before serving.

Asian-Style Pork with Noodles

2½-lb (1.25-kg) boneless pork shoulder, trimmed of most fat and cut crosswise into 3 or 4 pieces, each about 1 inch (2.5 cm) thick

Salt and freshly ground pepper

2 tablespoons olive oil

1 large yellow onion, finely chopped

4 cloves garlic, smashed

¼ cup (2 fl oz/60 ml) sake, beer, or dry white wine

½ cup (4 fl oz/125 ml) chicken stock, homemade (page 214) or purchased

2 large carrots, peeled and finely chopped

1 lb (500 g) fresh Chinese egg noodles

1 red bell pepper, seeded and thinly sliced

1 small red serrano chile, seeded and minced (optional)

⅓–½ cup (3–4 fl oz/80–125 ml) Asian Lime Vinaigrette (page 216)

¼ cup (⅓ oz/10 g) *each* chopped fresh cilantro and fresh flat-leaf parsley leaves

MAKES 6 SERVINGS

Season the pork all over with salt and pepper. In a large frying pan over medium-high heat, warm the oil. When the oil is hot, working in batches to avoid crowding, add the pork and sear, turning once, until golden brown on both sides, about 8 minutes total. Transfer the pork to a plate.

Pour off most of the fat from the pan and return to medium-high heat. Add the onion and sauté until softened and lightly golden, 6–8 minutes. Add the garlic and cook for 1 minute more. Pour in the sake and stir to dislodge any browned bits on the pan bottom. Stir in the stock and transfer the contents of the pan to a slow cooker. Add the carrots and place the pork and any accumulated juices on top. Cover and cook on the low setting for 5 hours. The meat should be very tender.

Transfer the pork to a platter and let rest for a few minutes. Meanwhile, using a large spoon, skim off as much fat from the braising liquid as possible. Shred the pork with 2 forks, then return it to the braising liquid.

Bring a saucepan three-fourths full of salted water to a boil. Add the noodles, stir, and cook until al dente, according to package directions. Drain well and transfer to a large bowl. Add the bell pepper, chile (if using), vinaigrette to taste, half each of the cilantro and parsley, about two-thirds of the shredded pork, and a generous amount of the tasty braising liquid. Toss to mix well.

Transfer to a platter and arrange the remaining pork, cilantro, and parsley over the top. Serve warm or at room temperature.

This sophisticated version of chow mein has been reinvented as a spicy noodle salad. The flavors are best when the dish is served at room temperature, making it an ideal candidate for a picnic. Complete the menu with sliced cucumbers tossed with a dressing of rice vinegar, Asian sesame oil, and sugar, and accompany with ice-cold Japanese beer.

Sweet & Sour Pork Loin with Figs

2 lb (1 kg) boneless pork loin roast, about 4 inches (10 cm) in diameter, trimmed of most fat

Salt and freshly ground pepper

3 tablespoons olive oil

½ large yellow onion, thinly sliced

4 cloves garlic, smashed

⅓ cup (3 fl oz/80 ml) dry white wine

2 tablespoons balsamic vinegar

½ cup (4 fl oz/125 ml) chicken stock, homemade (page 214) or purchased

2 tablespoons honey

About 12 fresh figs, stemmed and halved lengthwise

⅛ teaspoon ground cinnamon

1 cup (1 oz/30 g) baby arugula

2 tablespoons coarsely chopped pistachios (optional)

MAKES 4–6 SERVINGS

Season the pork generously all over with salt and pepper. In a large, heavy frying pan over medium-high heat, warm 2 tablespoons of the oil. Add the pork and sear, turning as needed, until golden brown on all sides, about 8 minutes total. Transfer the pork to a plate.

Pour off most of the fat from the pan and return it to medium-high heat. Add the onion and sauté until golden brown, about 8 minutes. Add the garlic and cook for 1 minute more. Pour in the wine and vinegar and stir to dislodge any browned bits on the pan bottom. Stir in the stock and honey, and then transfer the contents of the pan to a slow cooker. Place the pork on top. Cover and cook on the low setting for 6–7 hours. The pork should be very tender.

About 30 minutes before the pork has finished cooking, preheat the oven to 425°F (220°C). In a small roasting pan, toss the figs with the remaining 1 tablespoon olive oil, season with salt and pepper, and dust with the cinnamon. Roast, tossing halfway through the cooking, until softened and lightly golden, about 12 minutes.

Transfer the pork to a plate and let rest for few minutes. If the braising liquid appears to have a lot of fat, let it stand for a few minutes, then skim off the fat with a large spoon.

Slice the pork across the grain and divide among warm individual plates. Accompany each serving with a generous spoonful of the braising liquid. Top with the roasted figs and the arugula, and garnish with the pistachios, if using. Serve at once.

Keep this Italian-inspired dish in mind whenever fresh figs are in season. The sweet roasted fruits contribute a decadent flavor to the braised pork. Good-quality aged balsamic vinegar is luscious but can be expensive; fortunately a little goes a long way. For a complete meal, accompany the dish with roasted sweet potatoes or winter squash.

Braised Pork Chops with Peaches

6 bone-in pork loin chops, each about 1½ inches (4 cm) thick

Salt and freshly ground pepper

2 tablespoons olive oil

2 slices Canadian bacon, finely chopped

1 large yellow onion, halved and thinly sliced

6 cloves garlic, sliced lengthwise

½ cup (4 fl oz/125 ml) pale ale or lager

½ cup (4 fl oz/125 ml) chicken stock, homemade (page 214) or purchased

2 tablespoons cider vinegar or white wine vinegar

Arugula and Peach Salad for serving (see note)

MAKES 6 SERVINGS

Season the pork chops generously on both sides with salt and pepper. In a large, heavy frying pan over medium-high heat, warm the oil. When the oil is hot, working in batches if necessary to avoiding crowding, add the chops and sear, turning once, until golden brown on both sides, 8–10 minutes total. Transfer the chops to a plate.

Pour off all the fat from the pan and return it to medium-high heat. Add the bacon and onion and sauté until they begin to brown, 7–8 minutes. Add the garlic, then pour in the ale and stir to dislodge any browned bits from the pan bottom. Stir in the stock, vinegar, ¼ teaspoon salt, and several grinds of pepper, and then transfer the contents of the pan to a slow cooker. Stack the pork chops on top. Cover and cook on the low setting for 7 hours. The chops should be tender.

Transfer the pork chops to warm individual plates and spoon some of the braising liquid over the chops. Mound the salad on top of or alongside the pork chops. Serve at once.

ADD FRESHNESS WITH **ARUGULA AND PEACH SALAD**   In a bowl, whisk together 1½ tablespoons white wine vinegar, 1 teaspoon Dijon mustard, ¼ teaspoon salt, and several grinds of pepper. Whisk in ¼ cup (2 fl oz/60 ml) extra-virgin olive oil. Add 5 cups (5 oz/155 g) baby arugula and toss to coat. Add 4 peaches, pitted and thinly sliced, and toss gently to mix. Serve the salad at once.

Ale-Braised Sausages with Broccoli Rabe

6 fresh sweet Italian pork sausages, about 1¾ lb (875 g) total weight

2 large leeks, including the light green tops, halved and thinly sliced crosswise

2 small red bell peppers, seeded and sliced

3 bay leaves

Salt and freshly ground pepper

1 cup (8 fl oz/250 ml) plus 2 tablespoons brown ale or lager

2 teaspoons red wine vinegar

1 tablespoon olive oil

1 large bunch broccoli rabe, about 1 lb (500 g), tough ends removed and coarsely chopped

2 cloves garlic, finely chopped

¼ teaspoon red pepper flakes

MAKES 6 SERVINGS

Preheat the broiler. Arrange the sausages on a rack set in a rimmed baking sheet. Broil, turning as needed, until golden brown all over, 8–9 minutes total. Meanwhile, in a slow cooker, combine the leeks and bell peppers. Add the bay leaves, ½ teaspoon salt, and ½ teaspoon pepper.

When the sausages are ready, transfer them to the slow cooker, placing them on top of the vegetables. Drizzle with the 1 cup ale and the vinegar. Cover and cook on the low heat setting for 4 hours. The sausages should be cooked through and tender.

About 10 minutes before the sausages have finished cooking, in a large, heavy frying pan, warm the oil. Add the broccoli rabe and sauté just until it begins to color, 2–3 minutes. Add the garlic and pepper flakes and cook for 1 minute more. Reduce the heat to very low, add the remaining 2 tablespoons ale, and cover the pan. Cook until the broccoli rabe is tender but still bright green, about 5 minutes. Be careful not to overcook.

Divide the sausages among warm individual plates. Spoon the braising liquid around the sausages, pile the broccoli rabe on top, and serve.

The combination of brown ale, sweet fennel sausages, and hearty greens evokes chilly winter nights. Here, broccoli rabe adds a fresh, earthy, pleasantly sharp counterpoint to the hearty meal. Complete the menu with a loaf of crusty country bread and fresh fruit for dessert.

Red Wine–Braised Pork with Lentils

3-lb (1.5-kg) boneless pork shoulder, trimmed of most fat

Salt and freshly ground pepper

2 tablespoons olive oil

1 large yellow onion, finely chopped

2 stalks celery, finely chopped

4 cloves garlic, smashed

2 tablespoons dry red wine

½ cup (4 fl oz/125 ml) chicken stock, homemade (page 214) or purchased

1 large carrot, peeled and diced

Lentil and Endive Salad for serving (see note)

MAKES 6 SERVINGS

Season the pork generously all over with salt and pepper. In a large frying pan over medium-high heat, warm the oil. When the oil is hot, add the pork and sear, turning as needed, until golden brown on all sides, about 15 minutes total. Transfer the pork to a plate.

Pour off some of the fat from the pan and return it to medium-high heat. Add the onion and celery and sauté until softened and golden, about 10 minutes. Add the garlic and cook for 1 minute more. Pour in the wine and stir to dislodge any browned bits on the pan bottom. Stir in the stock and transfer the contents of the pan to a slow cooker. Add the carrot, and place the pork on top. Cover and cook on the low setting for 8–9 hours. The pork should be very tender.

Transfer the pork to a platter and let rest for a few minutes. Meanwhile, using a large spoon, skim the fat from the braising liquid. Cut the pork into slices across the grain, and then, if desired, shred with 2 forks. Spoon some of the braising liquid onto the meat to moisten.

Divide the lentil salad between warm individual plates and top with the pork. Spoon more of the braising liquid over the top, then serve.

ADD FRESHNESS WITH **LENTIL AND ENDIVE SALAD** Bring a saucepan three-fourths full of salted water to a boil. Add 1½ cups (10½ oz/330 g) green lentils, picked over and rinsed, and simmer over medium heat until tender but not mushy, about 30 minutes. Drain and rinse under cold running water until cool. In a bowl, toss together the cooked lentils; 2 heads Belgian endive, cored and sliced crosswise; 2 tablespoons coarsely chopped fresh flat-leaf parsley; ⅓–½ cup (3–4 fl oz/80–125 ml) Orange Vinaigrette (page 216); and ½ teaspoon ground cumin.

Garlicky Pork with Greens

2½-lb (1.25-kg) boneless pork shoulder, trimmed of most fat and cut into 1½-inch (4-cm) chunks

Salt and freshly ground pepper

2 tablespoons olive oil

1 large yellow onion, finely chopped

2 sprigs fresh thyme

15–20 cloves garlic

1 teaspoon minced fresh rosemary (optional)

⅔ cup (5 fl oz/160 ml) dry red wine

1 tablespoon red wine vinegar

⅔ cup (5 fl oz/160 ml) beef or chicken stock, homemade (page 214) or purchased

About 1¼ lb (625 g) kale, tough stems removed and leaves cut crosswise into wide strips

White Bean Salad for serving (see note; optional)

MAKES 6 SERVINGS

Season the pork generously with salt and pepper. In a large, heavy frying pan over medium-high heat, warm the oil. When the oil is hot, working in batches if necessary to avoid crowding, add the pork and sear, turning as needed, until well browned on all sides, 6–7 minutes total. Using a slotted spoon, transfer the pork to a plate.

Pour off most of the fat from the pan and return it to medium-high heat. Add the onion and thyme and sauté until the onion is golden brown, about 5 minutes. Add the garlic and rosemary and cook for 1 minute more. Pour in the wine and vinegar and stir to dislodge any browned bits on the pan bottom. Transfer the contents of the pan to a slow cooker. Add the stock and the pork and stir to combine. Cover and cook on the low setting for 5–6 hours, stirring two or three times during the first 2 hours if possible. Stir in the kale, re-cover, and cook for 30 minutes to 1 hour more. The pork and kale should be very tender.

Using a slotted spoon, divide the pork and kale among warm individual plates. Using a large spoon, skim away the fat from the braising liquid, then drizzle some of the liquid over the meat to moisten it. Top each serving with a large spoonful of the bean salad, if using. Serve at once.

ADD FLAVOR WITH **WHITE BEAN SALAD** In a bowl, combine 1 can (15 oz/470 g) white beans, rinsed and drained (or use about 2 cups/14 oz/440 g drained leftover cooked beans, page 191); 3 tablespoons extra-virgin olive oil; 1 tablespoon red wine vinegar; 2 tablespoons finely chopped fresh flat-leaf parsley; ¼ red onion, sliced paper-thin (about ¼ cup/1 oz/30 g); ¼ teaspoon salt; and several grinds of pepper. Stir well, then taste and adjust the seasoning.

Ginger Pork in Lettuce Cups

3-lb (1.5-kg) piece boneless
pork shoulder, trimmed
of most fat and cut into
3 large, uniform chunks

¼ cup (2 fl oz/60 ml) beef or
chicken stock, homemade
(page 214) or purchased

4 tablespoons (2 fl oz/60 ml)
low-sodium soy sauce

4 tablespoons (2 fl oz/60 ml)
dry sherry

Salt

4 whole star anise

4 thick slices fresh ginger,
unpeeled

1 can (8 oz/250 g) water
chestnuts, drained and
coarsely chopped

¼ cup (⅓ oz/10 g) coarsely
chopped fresh cilantro or
flat-leaf parsley

1–2 teaspoons rice vinegar

1–2 small heads butter lettuce

MAKES 8–10 SERVINGS

Place the pork in a slow cooker and add the stock. Drizzle the pork with 2 tablespoons each of the soy sauce and sherry, then sprinkle with ½ teaspoon salt. Cover and cook on the low setting for 2 hours. Turn the pork over, baste with the pan juices, re-cover, and cook for 2 hours more.

Turn the pork over and baste again. Drizzle the remaining 2 tablespoons each soy sauce and sherry over the pork and add the star anise and ginger. Re-cover and cook for 3–4 hours more, basting with the pan juices every hour or so if possible. The meat should be very tender.

Uncover, increase the setting to high, and cook until the braising liquid is slightly reduced, basting the pork frequently, about 30 minutes more. Using 2 forks, shred the pork while still in the slow cooker, mixing it with the braising liquid.

Using a slotted spoon, transfer the shredded pork to a bowl. Add the water chestnuts, cilantro, and rice vinegar to taste. Toss to mix well. Separate the butter lettuce into 12–20 whole, cuplike leaves. Mound a spoonful of the pork mixture into each lettuce cup and sprinkle with some cilantro. Arrange the lettuce cups on individual plates or a platter and serve at once.

Succulent ginger-braised pork shoulder is shredded and served in crisp lettuce leaves, for an appealing and fresh presentation. A splash of sweet rice vinegar and the addition of chopped water chestnuts fill every bite with bright crunch. These morsels make perfect appetizer-sized portions, and are also satisfying for a light meal.

Tangy Braised Pork Loin

2 lb (1 kg) boneless pork loin roast, about 4 inches (10 cm) in diameter, well trimmed

Salt and freshly ground pepper

2 tablespoons olive oil

2 large shallots, finely chopped

1 stalk celery, finely chopped

4 cloves garlic, smashed

⅓ cup (3 fl oz/80 ml) dry white wine

⅔ cup (5 fl oz/160 ml) chicken stock, homemade (page 214) or purchased

1 tablespoon white wine vinegar

Pear and Prosciutto Salad for serving (see note)

MAKES 6 SERVINGS

Season the pork generously all over with salt and pepper. In a large, heavy frying pan over medium-high heat, warm the oil. When the oil is hot, add the pork and sear, turning as needed, until golden brown on all sides, 8–10 minutes total. Transfer the pork to a plate.

Pour off most of the fat from the pan. Add the shallots and celery and sauté until golden brown, about 6 minutes. Add the garlic and cook for 1 minute more. Pour in the wine, stock, and vinegar and stir to dislodge any browned bits from the pan bottom. Transfer the contents of the pan to a slow cooker. Place the pork on the top. Cover and cook on the low setting for 6–7 hours. The meat should be very tender.

Transfer the pork to a platter and let rest for a few minutes. Meanwhile, using a large spoon, skim the fat from the braising liquid.

Slice the pork across the grain and divide among warm individual plates. Drizzle some of the braising liquid over the slices. Mound the pear salad alongside or over each serving. Serve at once.

ADD FRESHNESS WITH **PEAR AND PROSCIUTTO SALAD**   In a bowl, whisk together 1½ tablespoons white wine vinegar, 1 teaspoon Dijon mustard, ¼ teaspoon salt, and several grinds of pepper. Whisk in ¼ cup (2 fl oz/60 ml) extra-virgin olive oil. Add 3 just-ripe pears such as Comice or Bosc, cored and thinly sliced; 3 oz (90 g) thin-cut prosciutto, torn into strips; and 2 tablespoons finely chopped fresh flat-leaf parsley. Toss to mix.

Balsamic-Braised Sausages

1½ lb (750 g) fresh sweet or hot Italian pork sausages

1 large shallot, finely chopped

½ fennel bulb, cored and finely chopped

1 stalk celery, finely chopped

5 cloves garlic, smashed

Salt and freshly ground pepper

⅔ cup (5 fl oz/160 ml) chicken stock, homemade (page 214) or purchased

3 tablespoons balsamic vinegar

2 tablespoons dry white wine

2½ cups (15 oz/470 g) seedless red or green grapes, halved

1 bunch watercress, tough stems removed

⅓ cup (3 fl oz/80 ml) Shallot Vinaigrette (page 216)

MAKES 4 SERVINGS

Preheat the broiler. Arrange the sausages on a rack set in a rimmed baking sheet. Broil, turning as needed, until golden brown all over, 8–9 minutes total. Transfer the sausages to a plate.

In a slow cooker, stir together the shallot, fennel, celery, garlic, ½ teaspoon salt, and several grinds of pepper. Top with the broiled sausages and add the stock and balsamic and white wine vinegars. Cover and cook on the high setting for 2½ hours or on the low setting for 5½ hours, turning the sausages over halfway through if possible. The sausages should be tender and cooked through.

In a bowl, combine the grapes and watercress, drizzle with enough of the vinaigrette to coat lightly, and toss to coat evenly. Divide the sausages among warm individual plates, spoon some of the braising liquid around the sausages, and top with the grapes and watercress. Serve at once.

Be sure to use fresh sausages, rather than smoked ones, for this recipe. Browning them first in a broiler highlights their meaty flavor, and the slow cooker transforms them, making them meltingly tender. The fresh, robust flavors of the salad—tart-sweet grapes and peppery watercress—are the perfect counterpoint to the braised sausages. Large, dark purple grapes, which should be quartered rather than halved, are also lovely in this salad.

Carnitas

2-lb (1-kg) boneless
pork shoulder, trimmed
of some fat and cut into
1½-inch (4-cm) cubes

3 cloves garlic, finely chopped

2 teaspoons dried oregano,
preferably Mexican

1 teaspoon ground cumin

1 tablespoon sherry vinegar

Salt and freshly ground pepper

1 yellow onion, quartered

3 bay leaves

2 hearts of romaine lettuce,
thinly sliced crosswise

3 plum tomatoes,
seeded and diced

1 avocado, halved, peeled,
pitted, and cut into small dice

2 tablespoons coarsely
chopped fresh cilantro

2 limes, quartered

6–12 corn tortillas, each about
6 inches (15 cm) in diameter

Roasted tomato salsa for
serving, purchased (optional)

MAKES 6 SERVINGS

In a slow cooker, stir together the pork, garlic, oregano, cumin, vinegar, 1½ teaspoons salt, and several grinds of pepper. Add the onion and bay leaves, distributing them evenly in the mixture. Cover and cook on the low setting for 6 hours, stirring once halfway through if possible. The meat should be very tender.

Using a slotted spoon, transfer the pork to a plate. Remove and discard the onion and bay leaves. Using a large spoon, skim the fat from the braising liquid. Using 2 forks, shred the meat. Moisten the meat with just enough of the braising liquid to make it juicy. Keep warm.

In a bowl, combine the lettuce, tomatoes, avocado, and cilantro. Squeeze in the juice of ½ lime, season with salt and pepper, and toss to mix.

Heat a nonstick frying pan or a griddle over medium heat. One at a time, warm the tortillas, turning once, for about 30 seconds on each side. Wrap in a kitchen towel to keep warm until all have been heated.

For each serving, place 1 or 2 tortillas on each individual plate. Top the tortillas with equal amounts of the carnitas, the tomato-avocado salad, and the roasted tomato salsa, if using. Serve at once with the remaining lime wedges on the side.

This traditional Mexican dish of simmered pork is made with the well-marbled shoulder cut. Do not trim away all of the fat or the flavor of the dish will suffer. As the pork cooks, the fat is rendered and contributes to the richness of the pan juices. Served as tacos, the fresh topping of tomatoes, lettuce, and avocado provides the perfect counterpoint to the succulent meat.

Barbecue Baby Back Ribs

1 tablespoon bacon drippings or canola oil

½ yellow onion, finely chopped

3 cloves garlic, minced

1 cup (8 oz/250 g) ketchup

3 tablespoons Worcestershire sauce

3 tablespoons dry white wine

½ teaspoon grated lemon zest

1½ tablespoons lemon juice

1½ tablespoons firmly packed dark brown sugar

1½ teaspoons dry mustard

1½ teaspoons chipotle chile powder

1 teaspoon ground cumin

¼ teaspoon celery salt

Salt

⅛ teaspoon Tabasco or other hot pepper sauce, or to taste

5 lb (2.5 kg) baby back ribs

Apple-Fennel Slaw for serving (see note; optional)

MAKES 6 SERVINGS

To make the barbecue sauce, in a large, heavy saucepan over medium heat, warm the bacon drippings. Add the onion and garlic and sauté until softened, about 5 minutes. Stir in the ketchup, Worcestershire sauce, wine, lemon zest and juice, brown sugar, mustard, chile powder, cumin, celery salt, and ½ teaspoon salt. Bring to a simmer, then reduce the heat to low and cook very gently, stirring occasionally to prevent scorching, until slightly thickened, about 12 minutes. Stir in the Tabasco and taste for seasoning. Use right away, or preferably let cool, cover, and refrigerate for at least 24 hours before using.

Preheat the broiler. Trim the membrane from the back of each rack, then cut into individual ribs. Arrange the ribs on a rack set in a rimmed baking sheet. Broil, turning once, until browned on both sides, 10–12 minutes.

Transfer the ribs to a slow cooker, add the barbecue sauce, and turn the ribs to coat evenly. Cover and cook on the low setting for 5–6 hours. The ribs should be very tender.

Using a slotted spatula, transfer the ribs to a large platter and keep warm. Pour the sauce into a small saucepan, let stand for few minutes, and skim away the fat from the sauce with a large spoon. Bring to a boil over high heat and boil rapidly to reduce and thicken slightly, 3–4 minutes.

Arrange the ribs on warm individual plates and drizzle with some of the reduced sauce. If using, mound the slaw alongside the ribs. Serve at once.

ADD CRUNCH WITH APPLE-FENNEL SLAW In a large bowl, whisk together ¼ cup (2 fl oz/60 ml) each fresh lime juice, sour cream, and mayonnaise; ½ teaspoon each salt and chile powder, preferably chipotle; ¼ teaspoon sugar; and ¾ cup (¾ oz/20 g) fresh cilantro leaves, finely chopped. Add 2 large fennel bulbs, quartered lengthwise, cored, and thinly sliced crosswise; and 2 small tart red or green apples, peeled, cored, and thinly sliced. Toss to mix. Cover and refrigerate for 1 hour before serving to allow the flavors to marry.

Spicy Sausage & Mushroom Pasta

1½ lb (750 g) fresh hot Italian
pork sausages

1 large shallot, finely chopped

1 stalk celery, finely chopped

5 cloves garlic, smashed

½ teaspoon red pepper flakes

Salt and freshly ground pepper

2 tablespoons red wine

1 tablespoon red wine vinegar

⅔ cup (5 fl oz/160 ml)
chicken stock, homemade
(page 214) or purchased

¾ lb (375 g) fresh mushrooms
(see note), brushed clean
and cut into thick slices

1 lb (500 g) dried penne

Extra-virgin olive oil
for drizzling

¼ cup (1 oz/30 g) grated
pecorino romano or
Parmesan cheese

1 small bunch baby arugula or
watercress, tough stems
removed and coarsely chopped

MAKES 6 SERVINGS

Preheat the broiler. Arrange the sausages on a rack set in a rimmed baking sheet. Broil, turning as needed, until golden brown all over, 8–9 minutes total. Cut the sausages into 2-inch (5-cm) lengths.

In a slow cooker, stir together the shallot, celery, garlic, pepper flakes, ½ teaspoon salt, and several grinds of pepper. Top with the sausage pieces, and add the wine, vinegar, and stock. Cover and cook on the low setting for 4 hours, stirring once or twice if possible. Uncover, add the mushrooms, and continue cooking for 30 minutes more, stirring two or three times. The sausage pieces should be cooked through and the mushrooms tender.

About 15 minutes before the sausages and mushrooms are ready, bring a large pot three-fourths full of salted water to a boil, add the penne, stir, and cook until al dente, according to package directions. Drain the pasta.

In a warm serving bowl, combine the penne with the contents of the slow cooker and drizzle generously with olive oil. Sprinkle the cheese and arugula over the top, and serve at once.

Many different varieties of fresh mushrooms will work here, such as cremini, shiitake, or oyster. For a fresher, more concentrated flavor, instead of adding the mushrooms to the slow cooker, sauté them over medium heat in a little olive oil just until tender and browned, and then toss with the pasta and sausages. The arugula adds a pleasantly peppery flavor to the dish.

Moroccan Lamb Chops with Couscous

3 lb (1.5 kg) lamb shoulder chops, trimmed of most fat

¾ teaspoon ground cumin

Salt and freshly ground pepper

7 tablespoons (3.5 fl oz/110 ml) olive oil

1 large yellow onion, finely chopped

4 cloves garlic, smashed

¼ cup (2 fl oz/60 ml) dry red wine

½ cup (4 fl oz/125 ml) plus 1⅔ cups (13 fl oz/400 ml) chicken stock, homemade (page 214) or purchased

2 carrots, peeled and chopped

1¼ cups (7½ oz/235 g) quick-cooking couscous

1 cup (6 oz/185 g) diced dried apricots

2 tablespoons sherry vinegar

¼ cup (1 oz/30 g) sliced almonds, toasted (page 217)

¼ cup (⅓ oz/10 g) coarsely chopped fresh mint

MAKES 6 SERVINGS

Season the lamb generously all over with cumin, salt, and pepper. In a large frying pan over medium-high heat, warm 2 tablespoons of the olive oil. When the oil is hot, working in batches if necessary to avoid crowding, add the lamb and sear, turning as needed, until golden brown on all sides, 8–10 minutes total. Using a slotted spoon, transfer the lamb to a plate.

Pour off most of the fat from the pan and return it to medium-high heat. Add the onion and sauté until softened and lightly golden, 6–8 minutes. Add the garlic and cook for 1 minute more. Pour in the wine and stir to dislodge any browned bits on the pan bottom. Stir in the ½ cup stock and transfer to a slow cooker. Add the carrots and place the lamb and any accumulated juices on top. Cover and cook on the low setting for 8 hours. The meat should be very tender. Transfer the lamb to a plate. Let the braising liquid stand for a few minutes, then skim the fat from the liquid with a large spoon. Moisten the lamb with some of the liquid. Keep warm.

In a small saucepan over high heat, bring the 1⅔ cups stock to a boil and add ½ teaspoon salt. Remove from the heat. Put the couscous and apricots in a large heatproof bowl and stir in the hot stock. Cover the bowl and let stand for 5 minutes. The liquid should be absorbed. Fluff the couscous with a fork, add the remaining 5 tablespoons (3 fl oz/80 ml) olive oil, the vinegar, several grinds of pepper, and half each of the almonds and mint, and toss lightly to mix well.

Mound the couscous on a platter, arrange the lamb on top, and spoon some of the braising liquid over the lamb. Scatter with the remaining almonds and mint and serve at once.

Lamb shoulder chops, which are widely available, are well marbled, making them good candidates for braising in a slow cooker. Here, they are accompanied with couscous flecked with tangy dried apricots, to evoke a North African theme. To give the couscous a deeper flavor, use some of the defatted braising liquid from cooking the chops in place of the stock.

Lamb Shoulder with Salsa Verde

3-lb (1.5-kg) piece boneless lamb shoulder, trimmed of most fat and cut into 1¼-inch (3-cm) chunks

Salt and freshly ground pepper

2 tablespoons olive oil

1 large yellow onion, finely chopped

2 sprigs fresh thyme

4 cloves garlic, finely chopped

1 teaspoon dried oregano

⅔ cup (5 fl oz/160 ml) dry white wine or rosé

1 tablespoon balsamic vinegar

⅔ cup (5 fl oz/160 ml) beef or chicken stock, homemade (page 214) or purchased

Salsa Verde for serving (see note)

MAKES 6 SERVINGS

Season the lamb generously all over with salt and pepper. In a large, heavy frying pan over medium-high heat, warm the oil. When the oil is hot, working in batches if necessary to avoid crowding, add the lamb and sear, turning as needed, until well browned on all sides, 6–7 minutes total. Using a slotted spoon, transfer the lamb to a slow cooker.

Pour off most of the fat from the frying pan and return it to medium-high heat. Add the onion and thyme sprigs and sauté until the onion is golden brown, about 5 minutes. Add the garlic and oregano and cook for 1 minute more. Pour in the wine and vinegar and stir to dislodge any browned bits on the pan bottom. Transfer the contents of the pan to the slow cooker and add the stock. Cover and cook on the low setting for 8 hours. The lamb should be very tender.

Using a slotted spoon, divide the lamb among warm individual plates. Discard the braising liquid, which will be very fatty. Drizzle the salsa verde generously over the lamb. Serve at once.

ADD ZING WITH **SALSA VERDE** In a small food processor, combine 2 cloves garlic, chopped; 2½ cups (2½ oz/75 g) packed fresh flat-leaf parsley leaves; ½ cup (½ oz/15 g) packed fresh mint leaves; 2 tablespoons capers, rinsed and drained; 1 tablespoon Dijon mustard; and 1 tablespoon red wine vinegar. Pulse until finely chopped. With the processor running, drizzle in ⅔ cup (5 fl oz/160 ml) extra-virgin olive oil in a slow, steady stream and process until smooth. Cover and refrigerate for at least 1 hour for the flavors to marry before using. Use within 3–4 hours while it is still bright green.

Mediterranean Lamb Shanks

4–6 lamb shanks, about
1 lb (500 g) each,
trimmed of most fat

Salt and freshly ground pepper

2 tablespoons olive oil

1 large yellow onion,
finely chopped

2 cinnamon sticks

6 whole cloves

10 allspice berries

¼ cup (2 fl oz/60 ml) brandy

1 can (15 oz/470 g) diced
tomatoes, drained

½ cup (4 fl oz/125 ml)
beef stock, homemade
(page 214) or purchased

Israeli Couscous Salad
for serving (see note)

2 tablespoons coarsely
chopped fresh mint leaves

¼ cup (1 oz/30 g)
pomegranate seeds

MAKES 6 SERVINGS

Season the lamb shanks generously all over with salt and pepper. In a large, heavy frying pan over medium-high heat, warm the oil. When the oil is hot, working in batches if necessary to avoid crowding, add the shanks and sear, turning as needed, until golden brown on all sides, 8–10 minutes. Transfer the shanks to a slow cooker.

Pour off most of the fat from the pan and return it to medium-high heat. Add the onion, cinnamon sticks, cloves, and allspice and sauté until the onion is golden, about 7 minutes. Pour in the brandy and stir to dislodge any browned bits on the pan bottom. Stir in the tomatoes and stock, then pour the mixture over the lamb shanks. Cover and cook on the low setting for 8 hours. The meat should be very tender.

Transfer the shanks to a large plate. Strain the braising liquid into a small saucepan, let stand for a few minutes, and then skim away the fat with a large spoon. Bring to a boil over high heat and boil until reduced by about half, about 5 minutes. Pull the meat from the shanks and discard the bones. Leave the meat in chunks or shred with 2 forks.

To serve, mound the couscous salad in a large shallow serving bowl or platter. Top with the warm lamb, spoon some of the braising juices over the top, garnish with the mint and pomegranate seeds, and serve at once.

ADD FLAVOR WITH **ISRAELI COUSCOUS SALAD** In a saucepan over medium heat, warm 1 tablespoon canola oil. Add 1 small yellow onion, finely chopped, and sauté until softened, about 5 minutes. Add 1½ cups (8½ oz/265 g) Israeli couscous and stir until the couscous begins to brown, about 6 minutes. Add 2 cups (16 fl oz/500 ml) chicken stock, homemade (page 214) or purchased; ¾ teaspoon salt; and several grinds of pepper. Raise the heat to high and bring to a boil. Reduce the heat to medium-low, cover, and cook until the couscous is tender and all the liquid is absorbed, about 8 minutes. Transfer to a bowl, drizzle with ⅓–½ cup (3–4 fl oz/80–125 ml) Mint Vinaigrette (page 216), and fluff with a fork.

Braised Lamb Shanks with Sweet Peppers

4–6 lamb shanks, about 1 lb (500 g) each, trimmed of fat

Salt and freshly ground pepper

3 tablespoons olive oil

1 yellow onion, finely chopped

1 large carrot, peeled and finely chopped

1 stalk celery, finely chopped

3 bay leaves

1 teaspoon dried oregano

½ teaspoon ground cumin

½ cup (4 fl oz/125 ml) beef or chicken stock, homemade (page 214) or purchased

¼ cup (2 fl oz/60 ml) dry white wine

1 small yellow bell pepper, seeded and thinly sliced

1 small red bell pepper, seeded and thinly sliced

2 cloves garlic, finely chopped

3 tablespoons coarsely chopped fresh flat-leaf parsley

1 cup (5 oz/155 g) crumbled feta cheese

MAKES 4–6 SERVINGS

Season the lamb shanks generously all over with salt and pepper. In a large, heavy frying pan over medium-high heat, warm 2 tablespoons of the oil. When the oil is hot, working in batches if necessary to avoid crowding, add the shanks and sear, turning as needed, until golden brown on all sides, about 8 minutes total. Transfer to a plate.

Pour off most of the fat from the pan and return it to medium-high heat. Add the onion, carrot, celery, bay leaves, oregano, and cumin and sauté until the vegetables are golden, 6–8 minutes. Pour in the stock and wine and stir to dislodge any browned bits on the pan bottom. Transfer the contents of the pan to a slow cooker and stir in ½ teaspoon salt and several grinds of pepper. Place the lamb shanks on top. Cover and cook on the low setting for 7 hours, basting once or twice with the braising liquid if possible. The meat should be very tender.

Carefully transfer the shanks to a platter. Cover to keep warm. Strain the braising liquid into a small saucepan, let stand for a few minutes, then skim away the fat with a large spoon. Bring to a boil over high heat and boil until reduced by about half, about 5 minutes.

In a frying pan over medium-high heat, warm the remaining 1 tablespoon oil. Add the bell peppers and sauté until just beginning to soften, about 10 minutes. Add the garlic and cook for 1 minute more. Remove from the heat, stir in the parsley, and season with salt and pepper.

Divide the lamb shanks among warm individual plates and drizzle with the reduced braising liquid. Top each shank with a spoonful of the sautéed peppers. Sprinkle the feta over the top and serve at once.

Braised lamb shanks are an impressive and generous meal. If you like, remove the meat from the bones to serve an extra person or two. The topping of quickly sautéed peppers and crumbled feta adds tangy, fresh flavor and color to each serving. Accompany with orzo tossed with olive oil, finely chopped tomato, and minced fresh parsley.

POULTRY

Poultry is the perfect candidate for the slow cooker, where it can take its time becoming fall-off-the-bone tender. Here, the kitchens of France and Italy, Mexico and Morocco, Thailand and China contribute sweet, tart, and fiery flavorings to chicken, turkey, and duck, creating dishes that are both sophisticated and homey.

Chicken with Saffron Rice

Large pinch of saffron threads

½ cup (4 fl oz/125 ml) plus
3 tablespoons dry white wine

1 whole chicken, about 3½ lb
(1.75 kg), cut into 8 pieces
(2 thighs, 2 drumsticks,
2 breast-wing portions,
2 lower-breast portions)

Salt and freshly ground pepper

2 tablespoons olive oil

1 large yellow onion,
finely chopped

3 bay leaves

5 cloves garlic, finely chopped

1 teaspoon dried oregano

4 cups (32 fl oz/l l)
chicken stock, homemade
(page 214) or purchased

2 cups (14 oz/440 g)
long-grain white rice

2 large jarred roasted
pimiento peppers, seeded
and chopped (about
1½ cups/9 oz/280 g)

Warm Asparagus Salad for
serving (see note; optional)

MAKES 6–8 SERVINGS

Soak the saffron in the 3 tablespoons wine for 20 minutes. Oil the slow-cooker insert. Pat the chicken dry and season generously all over with salt and pepper. In a large, heavy frying pan over medium-high heat, warm the oil. When the oil is hot, working in batches to avoid crowding, add the chicken and sear, turning as needed, until golden brown, about 8 minutes total. Transfer the chicken to a plate.

Pour off most of the fat from the pan and return to medium-high heat. Add the onion and bay leaves and sauté until the onion is golden, about 5 minutes. Add the garlic and cook for 1 minute more. Add the oregano, ½ teaspoon salt, several grinds of pepper, the saffron mixture, and the remaining ½ cup wine and stir to dislodge any browned bits on the pan bottom. Add the contents of the pan and the stock to the slow cooker and then stir in the rice. Nestle the chicken in the rice, cover, and cook on the low setting for 3 hours.

Uncover and check to be sure a little liquid is still visible at the bottom of the cooker. If it appears dry, add 1 tablespoon water. Sprinkle the chopped pimiento evenly over the rice, then re-cover and cook for 15 minutes more.

Spoon the chicken and rice onto a large warm platter or individual plates and top with the salad, if using. Serve at once.

ADD FRESHNESS WITH **WARM ASPARAGUS SALAD** Trim the tough stem ends from 1 lb (500 g) asparagus, peel the lower 2 inches (5 cm) with a vegetable peeler, then cut the spears into 1½-inch (4-cm) lengths. Bring a saucepan three- fourths full of salted water to a boil over high heat. Add all the asparagus pieces except the tips and cook for 4 minutes. Add the tips and cook until all the pieces are just tender, about 2 minutes longer. Drain well. In a bowl, combine the warm asparagus, 1½ tablespoons fresh flat-leaf parsley leaves, and 2 tablespoons capers, rinsed. Drizzle with ⅓–½ cup (3–4 fl oz/80–125 ml) Lemon Vinaigrette (page 216) to coat lightly and toss well. Serve at once.

Italian Chicken Stew

Large pinch of saffron threads

⅓ cup (3 fl oz/80 ml) plus 3 tablespoons dry white wine

1 whole chicken, about 3½ lb (1.75 kg), cut into 10 pieces (2 thighs, 2 drumsticks, 2 wings, 4 breast portions)

¾ cup (4 oz/125 g) flour

Salt and freshly ground pepper

1 tablespoon olive oil

1 yellow onion, finely chopped

1 stalk celery, finely chopped

10 cloves garlic, smashed

⅓ cup (3 fl oz/80 ml) chicken stock, homemade (page 214) or purchased

1 can (28 oz/875 g) diced tomatoes, drained

3 bay leaves

1½ teaspoons red or white wine vinegar

Crostini with Red Pepper Aioli for serving (see note; optional)

2 teaspoons finely chopped fresh flat-leaf parsley

MAKES 6 SERVINGS

Soak the saffron in the 3 tablespoons white wine for about 20 minutes. Meanwhile, pat the chicken pieces dry. In a plastic bag, combine the flour, ¾ teaspoon salt, and several grinds of pepper. One at a time, add the chicken pieces and toss to coat evenly. Remove the chicken from the bag, tapping off the excess flour. In a large, heavy frying pan over medium-high heat, warm the oil. When the oil is hot, working in batches to avoid crowding, add the chicken and sear, turning as needed, until golden brown, about 8 minutes total. Transfer the chicken to a plate.

Pour off most of the fat from the pan and return it to medium heat. Add the onion and celery and sauté until softened and lightly golden, about 5 minutes. Add the garlic and cook for 1 minute more. Pour in the remaining ⅓ cup wine and the stock and stir to dislodge any browned bits on the pan bottom. Bring to a rapid simmer and cook to reduce slightly and to concentrate the flavor, about 10 minutes. Transfer the contents of the pan to a slow cooker and stir in the tomatoes, the saffron mixture, and the bay leaves. Stack the chicken on top. Cover and cook on the low setting for 5–6 hours. The chicken should be very tender.

Using a slotted spoon, transfer the chicken to a plate and keep warm. Remove and discard the bay leaves and stir the vinegar into the braising liquid. Let stand for a few minutes, then skim away the fat from the surface with a large spoon.

Divide the chicken evenly among shallow bowls and ladle some of the braising liquid and vegetables over each portion. Top each serving with a few crostini, if desired, and garnish with the parsley. Serve at once.

ADD CRUNCH WITH **CROSTINI WITH RED PEPPER AIOLI** In a small food processor, combine ⅔ cup (5 fl oz/160 ml) mayonnaise; 2 cloves garlic, minced; 1 small jarred roasted red pepper, well drained; and ½ teaspoon white wine vinegar. Pulse until smooth. Season with salt and freshly ground pepper, then fold in 2 teaspoons finely chopped fresh flat-leaf parsley. Top 12–18 Crostini (page 216) with a dollop of the aioli.

Garlicky Chicken Thighs

3 lb (1.5 kg) skin-on, bone-in chicken thighs, trimmed of excess skin and fat

Salt and freshly ground pepper

2 tablespoons olive oil

½ yellow onion, finely chopped

15 cloves garlic, peeled but left whole

2 sprigs fresh thyme

3 bay leaves

⅓ cup (3 fl oz/80 ml) dry white wine

1 teaspoon white wine vinegar

Shaved Fennel Salad for serving (see note; optional)

MAKES 6 SERVINGS

Pat the chicken thighs dry and season generously with salt and pepper. In a large, heavy frying pan over medium-high heat, warm the oil. When the oil is hot, working in batches to avoid crowding, add the chicken, skin side down, and sear until golden brown, about 4 minutes. Do not turn. Transfer the chicken to paper towels to drain briefly, then transfer to a slow cooker.

Pour off most of the fat from the pan and return it to medium-high heat. Add the onion, garlic, thyme, and bay leaves and sauté until the vegetables are just beginning to color, about 4 minutes. Pour in the wine and vinegar and stir to dislodge any browned bits on the pan bottom. Transfer the contents of the pan to the slow cooker. Cover and cook on the low setting for about 3 hours. The chicken should be very tender.

Transfer the chicken thighs to a plate and keep warm. Remove and discard the bay leaves and thyme sprigs. Strain the braising liquid into a small saucepan, reserving the whole garlic cloves. Let stand for a few minutes, and then skim away the fat with a large spoon. Bring to a boil over high heat and boil until slightly reduced and syrupy, about 5 minutes.

Divide the thighs among warm individual plates. Spoon the braising liquid and garlic cloves (the cloves will become sweet and nutty) over the chicken, and top with the fennel salad, if using. Serve at once.

ADD FRESHNESS WITH **SHAVED FENNEL SALAD** Cut off the stem and feathery tops and any bruised outer stalks from 2 fennel bulbs; chop the feathery tops to yield 2 tablespoons and reserve. Quarter each fennel bulb lengthwise, then core and cut crosswise into paper-thin slices. In a bowl, combine the fennel, fennel fronds, and 3 tablespoons chopped fresh flat-leaf parsley leaves. Drizzle with ⅓–½ cup (3–4 fl oz/80–125 ml) Lemon Vinaigrette (page 216) and toss well.

Braised Duck Legs

6 whole duck legs, 3–4 lb
(1.5–2 kg) total weight,
trimmed of excess skin and fat

Salt and freshly ground pepper

1 large yellow onion,
finely chopped

2 carrots, peeled and
finely chopped

2 stalks celery, finely chopped

½ cup (4 fl oz/125 ml) apple
juice, preferably unfiltered

2 teaspoons cider vinegar

¾ cup (6 fl oz/180 ml)
chicken stock, homemade
(page 214) or purchased

3 bay leaves

1 teaspoon juniper berries
(optional)

1 head frisée, torn into
bite-size pieces

Apple–Celery Root Salad
for serving (see note)

MAKES 6 SERVINGS

Preheat the broiler. Season the duck legs generously all over with salt and pepper. Arrange the duck legs on a rack set in a rimmed baking sheet. Broil, turning once, until golden brown on both sides, about 15 minutes total.

Transfer the duck legs, skin side up, to a slow cooker. Transfer 1 tablespoon of the rendered fat from the baking sheet to a large, heavy frying pan; discard the remaining fat or reserve for another use. Place the pan over medium-high heat. Add the onion, carrots, and celery and sauté until softened and just beginning to brown, about 7 minutes. Pour in the apple juice and vinegar and stir to dislodge any browned bits on the pan bottom. Stir in the stock, bay leaves, juniper berries, if using, ¼ teaspoon salt, and several grinds of pepper, and transfer the contents of the pan to the slow cooker. Cover and cook on the low setting for 6 hours. The duck legs should be very tender.

Transfer the duck legs to a plate. Pull off the skin, remove the meat from the bones, and discard the skin and bones. Shred the meat with 2 forks. Moisten the duck meat with a little of the braising juices.

To serve, make a bed of frisée on each plate, top with the apple–celery root salad, arrange the shredded duck on top, and garnish with the reserved green onion from the salad. Serve at once.

ADD CRUNCH WITH **APPLE–CELERY ROOT SALAD** Thinly slice 8 green onions, including the light green tops; set aside 2 tablespoons for garnish and place the remainder in a large bowl. Add 2 tablespoons cider vinegar; 2 teaspoons prepared horseradish, or to taste; and 3 tablespoons *each* extra-virgin olive oil and mayonnaise to the bowl and whisk together. Add 3 Granny Smith or other tart green apples, peeled, cored, and diced; and 1 small celery root, about ½ lb (250 g), peeled and shredded on the large holes of a box grater. Mix together until evenly coated.

Chicken & Coconut Curry

½ red onion, coarsely chopped

6 cloves garlic

1 tablespoon Thai
red curry paste

Grated zest and juice of 2 limes

1 tablespoon plus 1 teaspoon
Asian fish sauce

Salt and freshly ground pepper

5 lb (2.5 kg) skinless,
bone-in chicken thighs,
trimmed of excess fat

2 tablespoons plus
2 teaspoons canola oil

1 cup (8 fl oz/250 ml)
chicken stock, homemade
(page 214) or purchased

1¾ cups (14 fl oz/440 ml)
coconut milk

½ lb (250 g) green beans,
trimmed and coarsely chopped

1 small red bell pepper, seeded
and cut into matchsticks

½ teaspoon Asian sesame oil

½ cup (¾ oz/20 g) coarsely
chopped Thai basil or mint

Steamed jasmine rice
for serving

¼ cup (1 oz/30 g) unsweetened
shredded dried coconut,
toasted (page 217)

MAKES 4–6 SERVINGS

In a food processor, combine the onion, garlic, curry paste, the lime zest and juice, the 1 tablespoon fish sauce, ¼ teaspoon salt, and several grinds of pepper. Pulse until a chunky purée forms. Set aside.

Pat the chicken thighs dry. Season with salt and pepper. In a large, heavy frying pan over medium-high heat, warm the 2 tablespoons canola oil. When the oil is hot, working in batches if necessary to avoid crowding, add the chicken and sear, turning once, until golden brown on both sides, about 8 minutes total. Transfer the chicken to a slow cooker.

Reduce the heat to medium, add the curry mixture, and sauté, stirring often, until fragrant, about 4 minutes. Whisk in the stock and coconut milk and then bring to a simmer. Transfer to the slow cooker. Cover and cook on the low setting for 4 hours. The chicken should be very tender.

Using a slotted spoon, transfer the chicken pieces to a plate. Remove the meat from the bones, and discard the bones. Chop or shred the meat. Return the chicken meat to the slow cooker.

Meanwhile, bring a saucepan three-fourths full of salted water to a boil. Add the green beans and cook until crisp-tender, 3–4 minutes. Drain and rinse under cold running water. Stir the beans into the slow cooker, re-cover, and warm through for about 5 minutes.

In a frying pan over medium-high heat, warm the remaining 2 teaspoons canola oil. Add the red pepper and stir and toss until glossy and beginning to wilt, 1–2 minutes. Remove from the heat, add the remaining 1 teaspoon fish sauce, the sesame oil, and the basil and toss to mix well.

Spoon the rice into warm shallow bowls and top with the curry. Garnish with the red pepper mixture and toasted coconut and serve at once.

Thai curries pack an abundance of balanced flavors. Here, tender-crisp green beans, slivers of red bell pepper, and fresh basil join tender chicken thighs in an aromatic, light sauce, infused with creamy coconut milk. Serve with warm, steamed jasmine rice.

Provençal Chicken

1 whole chicken, about 3½ lb (1.75 kg), cut into 8 pieces (2 thighs, 2 drumsticks, 2 breast-wing portions, and 2 lower-breast portions)

Salt and freshly ground pepper

2 tablespoons olive oil, plus more for drizzling

½ large yellow onion, finely chopped

3 bay leaves

5 cloves garlic, finely chopped

1 teaspoon dried tarragon

½ cup (4 fl oz/125 ml) dry white wine

½ cup (4 fl oz/125 ml) chicken stock, homemade (page 214) or purchased

4 cups (4 oz/125 g) baby arugula

Fig and Olive Tapenade (see note) or purchased tapenade for serving

MAKES 6 SERVINGS

Pat the chicken dry. Season the chicken generously all over with salt and pepper. In a large, heavy frying pan over medium-high heat, warm the oil. When the oil is hot, working in batches to avoid crowding, add the chicken and sear, turning as needed, until golden brown, about 8 minutes total. Transfer the chicken to a plate.

Pour off most of the fat from the pan and return it to medium-high heat. Add the onion and bay leaves and sauté until the onion is golden, about 5 minutes. Add the garlic and cook for 1 minute more. Stir in the tarragon, ½ teaspoon salt, and several grinds of pepper. Pour in the wine and stock and stir to dislodge any browned bits on the pan bottom. Transfer the contents of the pan to a slow cooker and stack the chicken on top. Cover and cook on the low setting for 3 hours. The chicken should be tender.

Transfer the chicken to a plate and keep warm. Remove and discard the bay leaves. Strain the braising liquid into a small saucepan, let stand for a few minutes, and then skim away the fat with a large spoon. Bring to a boil over high heat and boil until reduced by about half to concentrate the flavors, about 10 minutes.

In a bowl, drizzle the arugula with a little olive oil, season with salt and pepper, and toss. Divide the chicken among warm individual plates and drizzle with the braising liquid. Top each portion with a large spoonful of tapenade and some of the arugula. Serve at once.

ADD FLAVOR WITH **FIG AND OLIVE TAPENADE** In a food processor, combine 1 cup (5 oz/155 g) *each* pitted mild green olives such as Picholine or Lucques and black olives such as Niçoise; 2 dried brown figs such as Brown Turkey, stemmed and chopped; 2 cloves garlic, chopped; 2 tablespoons extra-virgin olive oil; 2 teaspoons brandy; 1 teaspoon grated lemon zest; and ¼ teaspoon minced fresh rosemary. Pulse to form a chunky tapenade.

Chicken-Tortilla Soup

1 can (15 oz/470 g) tomato purée or crushed tomatoes

1 yellow onion, coarsely chopped

3 cloves garlic, smashed

1–2 jalapeño chiles, seeded and chopped

5½ cups (44 fl oz/1.4 l) chicken stock, homemade (page 214) or purchased

2 lb (1 kg) skinless, bone-in chicken thighs, trimmed of excess fat

3 limes

1 teaspoon red wine vinegar

1 teaspoon ground cumin

3 bay leaves

Salt and freshly ground pepper

2½ cups (15 oz/470 g) corn kernels (from about 5 ears)

2 small avocados, halved, pitted, peeled, and diced

2 tablespoons coarsely chopped fresh cilantro

Tortilla chips for garnish

MAKES 6 SERVINGS

In a blender or food processor, combine the tomatoes, onion, garlic, jalapeño to taste, and 1 cup (8 fl oz/250 ml) of the stock and process until smooth. Pour into a slow cooker.

Add the chicken thighs, the remaining 4½ cups (36 fl oz/1.1 l) stock, the juice of 1 lime, the vinegar, cumin, bay leaves, ¾ teaspoon salt, and several grinds of pepper. Cover and cook on the low setting for 5 hours. The chicken should be very tender.

Transfer the chicken pieces to a plate. Remove the meat from the bones, and discard the bones. Chop or shred the meat. Using a large spoon, skim away the fat from the braising liquid. Return the chicken meat to the slow cooker. Add the corn kernels, cover, and cook on the low setting until tender, about 30 minutes more. Remove and discard the bay leaves.

Cut the remaining 2 limes into wedges. Ladle the soup into warm shallow bowls, distributing all the ingredients evenly. Garnish each bowl with some of the avocados, cilantro, and tortilla chips. Serve at once. Pass the lime wedges at the table.

Serve this zesty soup with a tossed green salad for an easy weeknight supper. The creamy avocado, sweet corn, and cilantro add a splash of color and fresh flavor and the tortilla chips deliver a pleasant salty crunch to the soup. If fresh summer corn is out of season, use thawed frozen corn kernels and reduce the cooking time to 15 minutes.

Curried Chicken Salad

3 lb (1.5 kg) skinless, bone-in chicken thighs, trimmed of excess fat

Salt and freshly ground pepper

2 tablespoons olive oil

½ yellow onion, chopped

2 tablespoons curry powder

⅓ cup (3 fl oz/80 ml) dry white wine

2 teaspoons white wine vinegar

⅓ cup (3 fl oz/80 ml) chicken stock, homemade (page 214) or purchased

6 tablespoons (3 fl oz/90 ml) mayonnaise

1 tablespoon sour cream or plain yogurt

2 tart green apples, peeled, cored, and finely diced

2 stalks celery, finely diced

1 head butter lettuce, torn into bite-size pieces

1 cup (4 oz/125 g) pecan pieces, toasted (page 217)

2 green onions, sliced

2 tablespoons chopped fresh flat-leaf parsley

MAKES 6 SERVINGS

Pat the chicken thighs dry. Season lightly all over with salt and pepper. In a large, heavy frying pan over medium-high heat, warm the oil. When the oil is hot, working in batches to avoid crowding, add the chicken and sear, turning as needed, until golden brown, about 8 minutes total. Transfer the chicken to a plate.

Add the onion to the frying pan and sauté over medium-high heat until golden, about 5 minutes. Add the curry powder, stir to make a paste, and cook, stirring, for about 1 minute. Pour in the wine and vinegar and stir to dislodge any browned bits on the pan bottom. Stir in the stock, ½ teaspoon salt, and a few grinds of pepper. Transfer the contents of the pan to a slow cooker, and stack the chicken on top. Cover and cook on the low setting for 5 hours. The chicken should be very tender.

Transfer the chicken to a plate. Discard the braising liquid. Remove the meat from the bones, and discard the bones. Chop or shred the chicken.

In a bowl, whisk together the mayonnaise and sour cream. Fold in the shredded chicken, apples, and celery. Season with salt and pepper.

Make a bed of lettuce on each plate. Mound the chicken salad on the lettuce, scatter the pecans over the top, and garnish with the green onions and parsley. Serve at once.

Both curry powder and crisp apples are classic partners for chicken, and here they are combined in a fresh, light salad tossed with a creamy dressing, perfect for a light supper or lunch. If you like, you can use purchased candied pecans in place of the toasted pecans.

Chicken with Lemon & Green Olives

3 lb (1.5 kg) chicken drumsticks, trimmed of excess fat

Salt and freshly ground pepper

4 tablespoons (2 fl oz/60 ml) olive oil

½ yellow onion, finely chopped

2 stalks celery, finely chopped

2 sprigs fresh thyme

3 bay leaves

5 cloves garlic, finely chopped

⅓ cup (3 fl oz/80 ml) dry white wine

¼ cup (2 fl oz/60 ml) chicken stock, homemade (page 214) or purchased

1 teaspoon white wine vinegar

3 small lemons

1¼ cups (7½ oz/235 g) green olives, pitted and finely chopped

⅓ cup (2 oz/60 g) finely chopped blanched almonds

2 tablespoons finely chopped fresh flat-leaf parsley

MAKES 6 SERVINGS

Pat the drumsticks dry, then season all over with salt and pepper. In a large, heavy frying pan over medium-high heat, warm 2 tablespoons of the oil. When the oil is hot, working in batches to avoid crowding, add the chicken and sear, turning as needed, until golden brown, about 8 minutes total. Transfer the chicken to a plate.

Pour off most of the fat from the pan and return it to medium-high heat. Add the onion, celery, thyme, and bay leaves and sauté until the vegetables are just beginning to color, about 5 minutes. Add the garlic and cook for 1 minute more. Pour in the wine, stock, and vinegar and stir to dislodge any browned bits on the pan bottom. Transfer the contents of the pan to a slow cooker and place the chicken on top. Cover and cook on the low setting for about 3 hours. The chicken should be very tender.

Transfer the drumsticks to a serving platter and cover to keep warm. Strain the braising liquid into a small saucepan, let stand for a few minutes, and then skim off the fat with a large spoon. Reheat over medium heat and keep warm.

Slice 1 lemon crosswise as thinly as possible, preferably with a mandoline or other manual vegetable slicer. Remove the seeds and finely chop the slices, rind and all. In a bowl, combine the chopped lemon, olives, almonds, and parsley. Stir in the remaining 2 tablespoons oil, a scant ¼ teaspoon salt, and a few grinds of pepper.

Cut the remaining 2 lemons into wedges. Drizzle some of the warm braising liquid over the chicken, top with the lemon-olive relish, and serve at once with the lemon wedges on the side.

In this budget-friendly dish, chicken drumsticks become luscious and tasty after a long stint in the moist environment of the slow cooker. Serving them with a piquant lemon and olive relish helps to cut the richness of the meat. Accompany with creamy mashed potatoes or a savory herbed rice pilaf for soaking up the flavorful juices.

Moroccan Chicken with Couscous

1 whole chicken, 3½ lb
(1.75 kg), cut into 8 pieces
(2 thighs, 2 drumsticks,
2 breast-wing portions,
2 lower-breast portions)

Salt and freshly ground pepper

2 tablespoons olive oil

½ large yellow onion,
finely chopped

3 bay leaves

5 cloves garlic, finely chopped

1 teaspoon ground cumin

½ cup (4 fl oz/125 ml)
dry white wine

½ cup (4 fl oz/125 ml)
chicken stock, homemade
(page 214) or purchased

Chickpea Couscous for
serving (see note)

1½ tablespoons coarsely
chopped fresh flat-leaf parsley

¼ cup (1 oz/30 g) sliced
almonds, toasted (page 217)

MAKES 6 SERVINGS

Pat the chicken dry. Season generously with salt and pepper. In a large, heavy frying pan over medium-high heat, warm the oil. When the oil is hot, working in batches to avoid crowding, add the chicken and sear, turning as needed, until golden brown, about 8 minutes total. Transfer the chicken to a plate.

Pour off most of the fat from the pan and return it to medium-high heat. Add the onion and bay leaves and sauté until the onion is golden, about 5 minutes. Add the garlic and cook for 1 minute more. Add the cumin, ½ teaspoon salt, several grinds of pepper, the wine, and the stock and stir to dislodge any browned bits on the pan bottom. Transfer the contents of the pan to a slow cooker and stack the chicken on the top. Cover and cook on the low setting for 3½ hours. The chicken should be tender.

Transfer the chicken to a plate and keep warm. Remove and discard the bay leaves. Let the braising liquid stand for a few minutes, and then skim away the fat with a large spoon.

If desired, remove and discard the chicken skin. Mound the couscous on a warm platter and top with the chicken. Spoon some of the braising liquid over the chicken and couscous. Garnish with the parsley and toasted almonds and serve at once.

ADD FLAVOR WITH **CHICKPEA COUSCOUS** In a small saucepan, combine 1¼ cups (10 fl oz/310 ml) chicken stock, homemade (page 214) or purchased, and ½ teaspoon salt and bring to a boil. Put 1¼ cups (7½ oz/235 g) instant couscous and ¾ cup (4½ oz/140 g) golden raisins in a large heatproof bowl, and stir in the hot stock. Cover the bowl and let stand until the liquid is absorbed, about 5 minutes. Fluff the couscous with a fork, and then fold in 1 can (15 oz/470 g) chickpeas, well drained; ⅓–½ cup (3–4 fl oz/80–125 ml) Lemon Vinaigrette (page 216); ½ teaspoon ground cumin; and 2 tablespoons chopped fresh flat-leaf parsley. Season to taste with salt and pepper.

Braised Chicken with Summer Orzo Salad

2 lb (1 kg) skinless, bone-in chicken thighs, trimmed of excess fat

Salt and freshly ground pepper

2 tablespoons olive oil

½ small yellow onion, finely chopped

2 sprigs fresh thyme

3 bay leaves

6 cloves garlic, finely chopped

¼ cup (2 fl oz/60 ml) dry white wine

1½ teaspoons white wine vinegar

¼ cup (2 fl oz/60 ml) chicken stock, homemade (page 214) or purchased

Summer Orzo Salad for serving (see note)

MAKES 6 SERVINGS

Pat the chicken dry. Season generously all over with salt and pepper. In a large, heavy frying pan over medium-high heat, warm the oil. When the oil is hot, working in batches to avoid crowding, add the chicken and sear, turning as needed, until golden brown, about 8 minutes total. Transfer the chicken to a plate.

Pour off most of the fat from the pan and return it to medium-high heat. Add the onion, thyme, and bay leaves and sauté until the onion is just beginning to color, about 5 minutes. Add the garlic and cook for 1 minute more. Pour in the wine and vinegar and stir to dislodge any browned bits on the pan bottom. Stir in the stock, ½ teaspoon salt, and several grinds of pepper. Transfer the contents of the pan to a slow cooker and stack the chicken on top. Cover and cook on the low setting for 4 hours. The chicken should be very tender.

Remove the chicken pieces from the braising liquid and let cool slightly, then remove the meat from the bones, and discard the bones. Shred the meat with 2 forks. Divide the orzo salad among warm individual plates, and arrange the chicken on top. Drizzle the chicken with a little of the braising juices and serve at once.

ADD FRESHNESS WITH **SUMMER ORZO SALAD** Bring a large saucepan three-fourths full of salted water to a boil over high heat. Add 1 lb (500 g) orzo, stir well, and cook until al dente, according to package directions. Drain. In a large bowl, whisk together ¼ cup (2 fl oz/60 ml) extra-virgin olive oil; 2 tablespoons white wine vinegar; 1 tablespoon pesto, homemade (page 215) or purchased; ½ teaspoon salt; and several grinds of pepper. Add the orzo and toss to coat evenly. Fold in 1½ cups (9 oz/280 g) cherry tomatoes, halved or quartered, and 2 cups (2 oz/60 g) baby spinach.

Spicy Thai Chicken Salad

1 whole chicken, about 3½ lb (1.75 kg), cut into 10 pieces (2 thighs, 2 drumsticks, 2 wings, 4 breast portions)

Salt and freshly ground pepper

2 tablespoons peanut oil

1 stalk lemongrass

½ large yellow onion, finely chopped

5 cloves garlic, sliced

¼ cup (2 fl oz/60 ml) dry white wine

¼ cup (2 fl oz/60 ml) Asian fish sauce

½ cup (4 fl oz/125 ml) chicken stock, homemade (page 214) or purchased

½ small serrano or jalapeño chile, seeded and minced

¼ cup (2 fl oz/60 ml) Asian Lime Vinaigrette (page 216)

4 green onions, thinly sliced

2 tablespoons coarsely chopped fresh cilantro

1 heart of romaine lettuce, chopped

Lime wedges for serving

MAKES 6 SERVINGS

Pat the chicken dry. Season generously all over with salt and pepper. In a large, heavy frying pan over medium-high heat, warm the oil. When the oil is hot, working in batches to avoid crowding, add the chicken and sear, turning as needed, until golden brown, about 8 minutes total. Transfer the chicken to a plate.

Trim the lemongrass stalk to the bulb portion, remove the tough outer leaves, and cut into thick slices. Pour off most of the fat from the pan and return it to medium-high heat. Add the lemongrass and onion and sauté until the onion is golden, about 5 minutes. Add the garlic and cook for 1 minute more. Pour in the wine, fish sauce, and stock and stir to dislodge any browned bits on the pan bottom. Stir in the chile, ¼ teaspoon salt, and several grinds of pepper, and transfer the contents of the pan to a slow cooker. Stack the chicken on top. Cover and cook on the low setting for 5 hours. The chicken should be very tender.

Transfer the chicken pieces to a plate and let cool slightly. Pull off the skin, remove the meat from the bones, and discard the bones and skin. Shred the chicken meat with 2 forks. (Strain the braising liquid and reserve for another use if desired.)

In a bowl, combine the shredded chicken, vinaigrette, green onions, and 1 tablespoon of the cilantro and toss well. Arrange the lettuce on a platter and top with the chicken mixture. Garnish with the remaining 1 tablespoon cilantro and accompany with the lime wedges. Serve at once.

Here, piquant chicken perfumed with lemongrass and garlic tops crisp romaine lettuce, resulting in a dish that is perfect for a light summer supper. Freeze the tasty braising liquid left over here and use it to give an Asian flavor to chicken noodle soup.

Chicken Jambalaya

3½ lb (1.75 kg) skin-on, bone-in chicken thighs, trimmed of fat

Salt and freshly ground pepper

2 tablespoons olive oil

3 oz (90 g) cooked ham, diced

1 large yellow onion, chopped

1 green bell pepper, seeded and diced

3 cloves garlic, finely chopped

1 teaspoon dried oregano

½ cup (4 fl oz/125 ml) white wine

1 can (15 oz/470 g) diced tomatoes, drained

4 cups (32 fl oz/1 l) chicken stock, homemade (page 214) or purchased

2 teaspoons red wine vinegar

2 cups (14 oz/440 g) long-grain white rice

2 cups (10 oz/315 g) shelled fresh or thawed frozen peas

½ lb (250 g) medium shrimp in the shell

6 green onions, sliced

2 tablespoons coarsely chopped fresh flat-leaf parsley

2 lemons, cut into wedges

MAKES 6 SERVINGS

Oil the slow-cooker insert. Pat the chicken dry. Season generously all over with salt and pepper. In a large, heavy frying pan over medium-high heat, warm the oil. When the oil is hot, working in batches to avoid crowding, add the chicken and sear, turning as needed, until golden brown, about 8 minutes total. Transfer the chicken to a plate.

Pour off most of the fat from the pan and return it to medium-high heat. Add the ham, yellow onion, and bell pepper and sauté until the vegetables start to color, about 7 minutes. Add the garlic and oregano and cook for 1 minute more. Stir in ½ teaspoon salt, several grinds of pepper, and the wine and stir to dislodge any browned bits on the pan bottom. Transfer the contents of the pan to the slow cooker. Add the tomatoes, stock, and vinegar, then stir in the rice. Nestle the chicken in the rice, cover, and cook on the low setting for 3 hours.

Uncover and check to be sure a little liquid is still visible at the bottom of the cooker. If it appears dry, add 1 tablespoon water. Scatter the peas and shrimp evenly over the top. Re-cover and cook until the shrimp are pink, the chicken is cooked through, and the rice is tender, 15–20 minutes more.

Transfer the contents of the cooker to warm individual plates or a platter and scatter the green onions and parsley over the top. Squeeze some lemon juice over the top and arrange the remaining lemon wedges around the rim of the plate or platter. Serve at once.

In this classic dish of New Orleans, both the chicken and the rice cook to a wonderfully tender finish. The peas and shrimp are added toward the end, emerging vividly colorful. A scattering of green onions and parsley added just before serving delivers a final fresh touch.

Braised Chicken Pappardelle

1 whole chicken, about 3½ lb
(1.75 kg), cut into 10 pieces
(2 thighs, 2 drumsticks,
2 wings, 4 breast portions)

1 cup (5 oz/155 g) flour

Salt and freshly ground pepper

1 tablespoon unsalted butter

1 tablespoon olive oil

1 yellow onion, finely chopped

2 carrots, peeled and
finely chopped

1 stalk celery, finely chopped

¾ cup (6 fl oz/180 ml)
dry white wine

¾ cup (6 fl oz/180 ml)
chicken stock, homemade
(page 214) or purchased

3 bay leaves

⅔ cup (5 fl oz/160 ml)
heavy cream

Grated zest of 1 lemon

2 teaspoons *each* coarsely
chopped fresh tarragon
and chervil or parsley

1 lb (500 g) dried pappardelle

MAKES 6 SERVINGS

Pat the chicken pieces dry. In a bag, combine the flour and ¾ teaspoon salt. One at a time, add the chicken pieces and toss to coat evenly. Remove from the bag, tapping off the excess flour. In a large frying pan over medium heat, melt the butter with the oil. When the fat is hot, working in batches to avoid crowding, add the chicken and sear, turning as needed, until golden brown, about 8 minutes total. Transfer to a plate.

Pour off most of the fat from the pan and return it to medium heat. Add the onion, carrots, and celery and sauté until softened and golden, about 5 minutes. Pour in the wine and stock and stir to dislodge any browned bits on the pan bottom. Bring to a simmer and cook to concentrate the flavor, about 10 minutes. Transfer the contents of the pan to a slow cooker and add the bay leaves. Stack the chicken pieces on top. Cover and cook on the low setting for 5–6 hours. The chicken should be very tender.

Transfer the chicken pieces to a plate. Pull off the skin, remove the meat from the bones, and discard the bones and skin. Shred the meat and set aside to keep warm. Remove and discard the bay leaves, and transfer the braising liquid to a saucepan. Bring the braising liquid a to a simmer over medium-high heat. Cook, uncovered, for 5 minutes, then whisk in the cream, ½ teaspoon salt, and a few grinds of pepper. Return to a simmer and cook until reduced slightly, about 5 minutes. Stir in the lemon zest and half of the tarragon; keep the sauce warm.

Bring a large pot of salted water to a boil. Add the pappardelle, stir well, and cook until al dente, according to package directions. Drain, transfer to a warm serving bowl, and add the sauce. Toss to coat evenly. Mix in the chicken, scatter the remaining herbs over the top, and serve at once.

Tender braised chicken tossed with a tarragon-cream sauce and ribbons of pappardelle makes for a delicious and decadent cold-weather meal. Look for an organic chicken for superior flavor. The addition of lemon zest and fresh herbs imparts a welcome burst of flavor to the dish.

Spicy Buffalo-Style Chicken

5 lb (2.5 kg) chicken drumsticks, trimmed of excess fat

Salt and freshly ground pepper

1 tablespoon olive oil

½ yellow onion, finely chopped

2 stalks celery, finely chopped

10 cloves garlic, chopped

2 chipotle chiles in adobo sauce, chopped

6 tablespoons (3 oz/90 g) tomato paste

½ cup (4 fl oz/125 ml) beer

½ cup (4 fl oz/125 ml) Crystal hot sauce, Frank's Redhot sauce, or other medium-spicy hot sauce

2 teaspoons rice vinegar

1 tablespoon firmly packed light brown sugar

Celery–Blue Cheese Salad for serving (see note; optional)

MAKES 6 SERVINGS

Pat the chicken thoroughly dry and season all over with salt and pepper. In a large, heavy frying pan over medium-high heat, warm the oil. When the oil is hot, working in batches to avoid crowding, add the chicken and sear, turning as needed, until golden brown, about 8 minutes total. Transfer the chicken to paper towels to drain briefly, then transfer to a slow cooker.

Pour off some of the fat from the frying pan and return it to medium-high heat. Add the onion and celery and sauté until just beginning to brown, about 5 minutes. Add the garlic, chiles, and tomato paste and cook, stirring, for 2 minutes more. Pour in the beer, hot sauce, and vinegar and stir to dislodge any browned bits on the pan bottom. Transfer the contents of the pan to the slow cooker. Cover and cook on the low setting for about 5 hours. The chicken should be tender.

Transfer the chicken to a plate. Using a large spoon, skim off the fat from the braising liquid. Transfer the liquid to a blender or food processor and process until smooth. Pour into a frying pan, place over medium heat, and stir in the brown sugar. Bring to a simmer and cook, stirring occasionally, until thickened and glossy, about 10 minutes. Return the drumsticks to the sauce and simmer until heated through, 3–4 minutes.

If using, divide the celery and blue cheese salad among individual plates. Arrange the drumsticks alongside the salad and serve at once, passing additional sauce at the table.

ADD FRESHNESS WITH **CELERY–BLUE CHEESE SALAD** Using a sharp knife, very thinly slice 3 celery hearts crosswise, including some of the leafy tops, and place in a bowl. Thinly slice 7 green onions, including the light green tops, and add to the bowl. Add the grated zest of 1 lemon, 1½ tablespoons fresh lemon juice, 3 tablespoons extra-virgin olive oil, and several grinds of pepper and toss well. Fold in ⅔ cup (3½ oz/105 g) crumbled blue cheese.

Turkey & White Bean Chili

2¼ cups (1 lb/500 g) dried Great Northern or other small white beans, picked over and rinsed

1 arbol, 1 or 2 serrano, or 1 jalapeño chile

3 bay leaves

6 cups (48 fl oz/1.5 l) chicken stock, homemade (page 214) or purchased

1 tablespoon canola oil

1 lb (500 g) ground dark-meat turkey

1 large yellow onion, finely chopped

Salt and freshly ground pepper

5 cloves garlic, minced

2 tablespoons chili powder

1½ tablespoons ground cumin

¼–½ teaspoon cayenne pepper (optional)

Sour cream for serving

6 green onions, finely chopped

⅓ cup (½ oz/15 g) coarsely chopped fresh cilantro

MAKES 6 SERVINGS

In a large bowl, combine the beans with water to cover by 2 inches (5 cm) and let soak overnight. Drain well and transfer to a slow cooker. Add the chile, bay leaves, and stock. The stock should cover the beans by about 1½ inches (4 cm); add water as needed to supplement. Cover and cook on the low setting for 6 hours. The beans should be tender.

In a large, heavy frying pan over medium heat, warm the oil. Add the turkey and cook, stirring to break it up, until the meat is no longer pink, 8–10 minutes. Add the onion, 1 teaspoon salt, and several grinds of pepper and sauté, stirring occasionally, until the onion is very soft and lightly golden, about 10 minutes. Add the garlic, chili powder, cumin, and cayenne to taste, if using, and stir together for 2–3 minutes to release their aromas. Transfer the contents of the pan to the slow cooker with the beans and increase the heat to the high setting. Cover and cook, stirring 2 or 3 times, until slightly thickened, 30–40 minutes. Taste and adjust the seasoning.

Ladle the chili into warm shallow bowls. Top each serving with a dollop of sour cream and garnish with the green onions and cilantro. Serve at once.

If you prefer chili with a smoother consistency, scoop out about 1 cup (7 oz/220 g) before you add the turkey mixture, process in a blender or food processor until smooth, and then stir the purée back into the chili. Don't skip on the garnishes—sour cream, green onion, and cilantro—which give this slow-cooked dish a welcome accent. Serve wedges of corn bread alongside.

Turkey Mole Tacos

2 ancho chiles

3 tablespoons canola oil

2 yellow onions, finely chopped

1 cup (4 oz/125 g) sliced almonds

2 tablespoons pure
chile powder

1½ teaspoons ground cumin

¾ teaspoon ground cinnamon

1 can (15 oz/470 g) diced
tomatoes, drained

2 oz (60 g) bittersweet
chocolate, chopped

1½ teaspoons dried oregano

Salt and freshly ground pepper

3 cups (24 fl oz/750 ml)
chicken stock, homemade
(page 214) or purchased

1 whole boneless, skinless
turkey breast, about 4 lb
(2 kg), cut into 2-inch
(5-cm) chunks

12–16 flour tortillas, 6 inches
(15 cm) in diameter, warmed

2 hearts of romaine lettuce,
shredded

6 green onions, including the
light green tops, finely chopped

8–10 oz (250–315 g) *queso fresco*
or farmer's cheese, crumbled

MAKES 6–8 SERVINGS

Seed the ancho chiles and tear them into flat pieces. In a frying pan over high heat, warm the oil. When the oil is hot, add the chiles and fry just until they begin to darken and release a pungent aroma, 15–20 seconds. Using tongs, transfer to a paper towel and set aside.

Reduce the heat to medium-high, add the onions and almonds, and sauté just until golden, 6–8 minutes. Stir in the chile powder, cumin, and cinnamon and sauté until aromatic, about 30 seconds longer. Stir in the tomatoes, chocolate, oregano, 2 teaspoons salt, 1 teaspoon pepper, and 1½ cups (12 fl oz/375 ml) of the stock. Continue stirring until the chocolate has melted, about 1 minute. Remove from the heat and let cool for 5 minutes.

Transfer the mixture to a food processor or blender, add the reserved chiles, and process until smooth; you may need to process in batches. Transfer the purée to a slow cooker and stir in the remaining 1½ cups stock. Add the turkey breast and turn to coat evenly. Cover and cook on the low setting for 4 hours, stirring once or twice if possible. The turkey should be very tender.

Using a slotted spoon, transfer the turkey to a wide, shallow bowl. Using 2 forks, shred the turkey and then add a generous amount of the mole sauce to bind it and make it juicy. (If desired, reserve the remaining mole sauce for another use; store in an airtight container in the refrigerator for up to 3 days or in the freezer for up to 3 months.)

Arrange the tortillas on a work surface and mound some of the shredded turkey in the center of each tortilla. Top each with some lettuce and green onion, and then with 1–2 tablespoons of the cheese. Roll the tacos up loosely, arrange on a warm platter, and serve at once.

Boldly-spiced mole has a reputation for being labor intensive, but this simplified version eliminates much of the work, while still rendering the dish's unmistakably complex flavor. Crisp romaine, a sprinkling of green onion, and tangy fresh cheese accent the dish.

Five-Spice Chicken Soup

2 lb (1 kg) skinless, boneless chicken thighs

Salt and freshly ground pepper

1 teaspoon five-spice powder

2 tablespoons peanut oil

1 yellow onion, finely chopped

5½ cups (44 fl oz/1.4 l) chicken stock, homemade (page 214) or purchased

Two 1-inch (2.5-cm) pieces fresh ginger, peeled

¼ cup (2 fl oz/60 ml) soy sauce

¼ cup (2 fl oz/60 ml) Asian fish sauce

1 tablespoon rice vinegar

¼ lb (125 g) rice stick noodles

2 tablespoons *each* chopped fresh basil and fresh cilantro

1 cup (3 oz/90 g) bean sprouts

½–1 small serrano or jalapeño chile, seeded and thinly sliced

Lime wedges for serving

MAKES 6 SERVINGS

Pat the chicken dry and season generously on all sides with salt and pepper and the five-spice powder. In a large, heavy frying pan over medium-high heat, warm the oil. When the oil is hot, working in batches to avoid crowding, add the chicken and sear, turning as needed, until golden brown, about 8 minutes total. Transfer the chicken to paper towels to drain briefly, then transfer to a slow cooker.

Add the onion to the frying pan and sauté over medium-high heat until golden, 6–7 minutes. Pour in 1 cup (8 fl oz/250 ml) of the stock and stir to dislodge any browned bits on the pan bottom. Transfer the contents of the pan to the slow cooker. Stir in the remaining 4½ cups (36 fl oz/1.1 l) stock, the ginger, soy sauce, fish sauce, and vinegar. Cover and cook on the low setting for 5 hours. The chicken should be very tender.

About 10 minutes before the soup is ready, place the noodles in a bowl with hot water to cover generously to rehydrate.

Transfer the chicken to a plate and remove and discard the ginger. Remove the meat from the bones, and discard the bones. Using 2 forks, shred the meat. Return the chicken meat to the soup. Drain the noodles and stir into the soup. Warm through for about 2 minutes on the high setting.

Ladle the soup into warm shallow bowls, distributing the chicken evenly. Scatter the basil, cilantro, bean sprouts, and chile over the top and place the lime wedges alongside. Serve at once.

The formula for aromatic five-spice powder, and sometimes even the spices, varies depending on the manufacturer, but it usually contains cloves, star anise, fennel, cinnamon, Sichuan pepper, and sometimes ginger. Here, it flavors a Southeast Asian–inspired soup that is topped with crunchy bean sprouts and fresh herbs just before serving.

Herbed Chicken with Zesty Potato Salad

3 lb (1.5 kg) skin-on, bone-in chicken thighs, trimmed of excess fat

Salt and freshly ground pepper

2 tablespoons olive oil

½ yellow onion, finely chopped

4 cloves garlic, smashed

2 sprigs fresh thyme

2 sprigs fresh oregano

3 bay leaves

⅓ cup (3 fl oz/80 ml) dry white wine

2 teaspoons white wine vinegar

⅓ cup (3 fl oz/80 ml) chicken stock, homemade (page 214) or purchased

Zesty Potato Salad for serving (see note; optional)

MAKES 6 SERVINGS

Pat the chicken thighs dry and season generously all over with salt and pepper. In a large, heavy frying pan over medium-high heat, warm the oil. When the oil is hot, working in batches to avoid crowding, add the chicken, skin side down, and sear until golden brown, about 4 minutes. Do not turn. Transfer the chicken to paper towels to drain briefly, then transfer to a slow cooker.

Add the onion, garlic, thyme, oregano, and bay leaves to the same pan and sauté over medium-high heat until the vegetables are just beginning to color, about 5 minutes. Pour in the wine and vinegar and stir to dislodge any browned bits on the pan bottom. Stir in the stock, ½ teaspoon salt, and several grinds of pepper, then pour the contents of the pan over the chicken. Cover and cook on the low setting for 4 hours. The chicken should be very tender.

Transfer the chicken to a plate and keep warm. Remove and discard the bay leaves and the thyme and oregano sprigs. Let the braising liquid stand for a few minutes, then skim off the fat with a large spoon.

Divide the chicken thighs among warm individual plates. Drizzle with some of the braising liquid. If using, mound the salad on top of or alongside the chicken. Serve at once.

ADD FRESHNESS WITH **ZESTY POTATO SALAD**   Quarter 20 small red potatoes, place in a large saucepan with salted water to cover, and bring to a gentle boil over medium-high heat. Cook, uncovered, until just tender, about 8 minutes. Drain, transfer to a serving bowl, drizzle with ⅓–½ cup (3–4 fl oz/80–125 ml) Shallot Vinaigrette (page 216) to coat lightly, and toss well. Let cool slightly, then add 2 cups (12 oz/375 g) cherry tomatoes, halved; and 1 tablespoon finely chopped fresh oregano. Toss to coat.

SEAFOOD

Meaty tuna, sweet monkfish, buttery salmon, and delicate cod all take deliciously to the slow cooker, where they are transformed into seductive stews and chowders. In this chapter, they are combined with such aromatic ingredients as fennel, saffron, smoked paprika, citrus, and a garden of herbs to create a diverse array of memorable main courses.

Braised Salmon with Green Beans

½ cup (4 fl oz/125 ml) vegetable stock, homemade (page 215) or purchased

1 cup (8 fl oz/250 ml) dry white wine

½ small yellow onion, sliced

3 sprigs plus 1 teaspoon minced fresh tarragon

Salt and freshly ground pepper

6 salmon fillets, each about 5 oz (155 g)

1 lb (500 g) haricots verts or green beans, trimmed

1 tablespoon unsalted butter

1 tablespoon olive oil

1 large shallot, minced

2 teaspoons white wine vinegar

MAKES 6 SERVINGS

In a slow cooker, stir together ½ cup (4 fl oz/125 ml) water, the stock, wine, onion, tarragon sprigs, ½ teaspoon salt, and several grinds of pepper. Cover and cook on the low setting for 30 minutes. Add the salmon fillets (they can overlap), re-cover, and cook for 1 hour. The fish should be opaque throughout, firm, and very tender.

About 10 minutes before the salmon is ready, bring a large saucepan three-fourths full of lightly salted water to a boil. Add the green beans and cook until tender-crisp, 4–5 minutes. Drain and hold under cold running water until cool. Spread on a kitchen towel to dry. In a frying pan over medium heat, melt the butter with the oil. Add the shallot and sauté until slightly softened, 2–3 minutes. Add the beans and stir until hot throughout. Add the vinegar and minced tarragon and toss to mix.

Transfer the salmon to warm individual plates. Discard the braising liquid or strain and reserve for another use. Arrange a mound of the green beans alongside each salmon fillet. Serve at once.

Highly nutritious salmon becomes melt-in-your-mouth tender after a short braise in the slow cooker. The haricots verts—slender green beans—are cooked just until tender then tossed with shallot and fresh tarragon, providing a brightly flavored counterpoint to the meaty fish.

Tuna with Herbed White Beans

½ cup (4 fl oz/125 ml)
vegetable stock, homemade
(page 215) or purchased

½ cup (4 fl oz/125 ml) dry
white wine or rosé

4 tablespoons olive oil

1 can (15 oz/470 g) diced
tomatoes, drained

½ small yellow onion,
finely chopped

3 sprigs fresh thyme

6 cloves garlic, finely chopped

Salt and freshly ground pepper

¾ lb (375 g) ahi tuna

1 can (15 oz/470 g) white
beans, rinsed and drained

1 tablespoon red wine vinegar

¼ red onion, thinly sliced

2 tablespoons chopped
fresh flat-leaf parsley

Grated zest of 1 lemon

MAKES 4 SERVINGS

In a slow cooker, stir together the stock, wine, 1 tablespoon of the olive oil, the tomatoes, yellow onion, thyme, garlic, ½ teaspoon salt, and several grinds of pepper. Cover and cook on the low setting for 30 minutes. Add the tuna, re-cover, and cook for 15–20 minutes. The tuna should be firm. After about 15 minutes, it will still be slightly pink at the center; after 20 minutes, it will be opaque throughout.

In a bowl, combine the beans, the remaining 3 tablespoons olive oil, the vinegar, red onion, half of the parsley, half of the lemon zest, ¼ teaspoon salt, and several grinds of pepper. Stir well, then taste and adjust the seasoning with more salt and pepper if needed.

Using a slotted spatula, transfer the tuna and vegetables to a plate. Discard the braising liquid. Using 2 forks, pull the tuna apart into flakes.

To serve, divide the white bean mixture among individual plates. Top the beans with the flaked tuna and vegetables, garnish with the remaining parsley and lemon zest, and serve.

Tuna and white beans are a classic combination, but this flavorful version takes the dish to a whole new level. The tender braised fish and creamy beans mix with the sparkling flavors of vinaigrette, fresh herbs, and lemon zest. This dish would make perfect picnic fare: pack the white bean salad and tuna in separate containers, and then combine them at the picnic site.

Smoky Whitefish & Potato Chowder

2 tablespoons unsalted butter

1 yellow onion, finely chopped

2 stalks celery, finely chopped

1 lb (500 g) red new potatoes, unpeeled

3½ cups (28 fl oz/875 ml) fish or vegetable stock, homemade (page 215) or purchased

⅔ cup (5 fl oz/160 ml) dry white wine

1 teaspoon dried tarragon

Salt and freshly ground pepper

½ lb (250 g) fresh sole or tilapia fillets

½ lb (250 g) smoked whitefish or smoked trout fillets

½ cup (3 oz/90 g) diced cooked ham

⅔ cup (5 fl oz/160 ml) heavy cream

1½ teaspoons white wine vinegar

Corn-Pepper Relish for serving (see note; optional)

MAKES 4–6 SERVINGS

In a large frying pan over medium heat, melt the butter. Add the onion and celery and sauté until softened, about 6 minutes. Transfer the contents of the pan to a slow cooker.

Cut the potatoes into ½-inch (12-mm) cubes and add to the slow cooker along with the stock, wine, tarragon, ½ teaspoon salt, and several grinds of pepper. Cover and cook on the low setting for about 6 hours. The potatoes should be tender.

Cut the sole into 1-inch (2.5-cm) pieces. Remove the skin from the smoked whitefish, discard the skin, and flake the whitefish into pieces. Add the sole, smoked whitefish, ham, and cream to the slow cooker, increase the setting to high, and cook for about 20 minutes more. The sole should be firm and opaque. Stir in the vinegar, then taste and adjust the seasoning.

Ladle the chowder into warm shallow bowls, distributing the fish and potatoes evenly. Top each portion with a spoonful of the warm relish, if using, and serve at once.

ADD FRESHNESS WITH **CORN-PEPPER RELISH** In a frying pan over medium-high heat, warm 1 tablespoon extra-virgin olive oil. Add 1½ cups (9 oz/280 g) fresh or thawed, frozen corn kernels and 1 red bell pepper, seeded and finely diced. Sauté until the vegetables are slightly softened and beginning to color, about 3 minutes. Season with salt and freshly ground pepper. Remove from the heat and stir in 2 tablespoons finely snipped fresh chives.

Braised Salmon with Cucumber-Yogurt Salad

½ cup (4 fl oz/125 ml) vegetable stock, homemade (page 215) or purchased

1 cup (8 fl oz/250 ml) dry white wine

½ small yellow onion, sliced

3 sprigs fresh dill, plus 4 tablespoons (⅓ oz/10 g) coarsely chopped fresh dill

Salt and freshly ground pepper

6 salmon fillets, each about 5 oz (155 g)

1 cup (8 oz/250 g) plain yogurt

1 tablespoon mayonnaise

1 shallot, minced

4 tablespoons (⅓ oz/10 g) coarsely chopped fresh flat-leaf parsley

¼ teaspoon ground cumin

1 English cucumber, halved lengthwise and thinly sliced crosswise

MAKES 6 SERVINGS

In a slow cooker, stir together ½ cup (4 fl oz/125 ml) water, the stock, wine, onion, dill sprigs, ½ teaspoon salt, and several grinds of pepper. Cover and cook on the low setting for 30 minutes to blend the flavors. Add the salmon, re-cover, and cook for 1 hour. The fish should be opaque throughout, firm, and very tender.

Meanwhile, in a bowl, whisk together the yogurt, mayonnaise, shallot, 3 tablespoons of the chopped dill, 3 tablespoons of the parsley, and the cumin. Add the cucumber and mix well. Season with salt and pepper.

Transfer the salmon fillets to warm individual plates. Discard the braising liquid. Spoon the cucumber-yogurt sauce over each salmon fillet. Garnish with the remaining dill and parsley, and serve at once.

The slow cooker reveals the succulent texture of salmon, a fish rich in healthy oils. These natural oils mean that a long, gentle cooking time makes the salmon surprisingly light and meltingly tender. Grassy dill, delicate cucumber, and tangy yogurt complete the palate.

Swordfish with Lemon-Caper Butter

½ cup (4 fl oz/125 ml) dry white wine

1 slice yellow onion

1 thick slice lemon

3 sprigs fresh dill, plus 2 teaspoons chopped fresh dill

3 bay leaves

Salt and freshly ground pepper

1 swordfish steak, about 1½ lb (750 g) and 1 inch (2.5 cm) thick, cut into 4 equal pieces

6 tablespoons (3 oz/90 g) unsalted butter, at room temperature

1 teaspoon grated lemon zest

2 tablespoons capers, rinsed and drained

MAKES 4 SERVINGS

In a slow cooker, stir together ½ cup (4 fl oz/125 ml) water, the wine, onion, lemon, dill sprigs, bay leaves, and ¼ teaspoon salt. Cover and cook on the high setting for 30 minutes.

Season the swordfish lightly on both sides with salt and pepper and place in the slow cooker. Re-cover and cook until tender, about 30 minutes.

Meanwhile, in a small food processor, combine the butter, lemon zest, capers, and chopped dill. Pulse to blend evenly. (Alternatively, finely chop together the capers and dill, combine with the butter and lemon zest in a small bowl, and mix together with a wooden spoon.)

Transfer the swordfish to warm individual plates. Discard the braising liquid. Top each portion of fish with a spoonful of the butter and serve.

This elegant dish requires no last-minute attention, leaving your hands free to create an appetizer or side dish that does. Meaty fish such as swordfish and salmon become beautifully tender in the moist atmosphere of the slow cooker yet retain their shape for an effort-free transfer from cooker to plate. A dollop of piquant, flavored butter, laced with lemon zest and capers, is a nice counterpoint to the dense flesh of the swordfish.

Simple Fish Bouillabaisse

2 tablespoons olive oil

10 cloves garlic, thinly sliced

1 tablespoon fennel seeds

3 bay leaves

¼ cup (2 oz/60 g) tomato paste

Salt and freshly ground pepper

⅓ cup (3 fl oz/80 ml) dry white wine

1 large fennel bulb

1 can (15 oz/470 g) crushed tomatoes, with juice

5 cups (40 fl oz/1.25 l) fish or vegetable stock, homemade (page 215) or purchased

2 lb (1 kg) fresh cod or monkfish fillets, cut into 2-inch (5-cm) chunks

Grated zest of 1 orange

2 tablespoons chopped fresh chervil (optional)

Crostini (page 216) for serving

MAKES 4–6 SERVINGS

In a large, heavy frying pan over low heat, warm the oil. Add the garlic, fennel seeds, and bay leaves and cook gently, stirring occasionally, until the garlic is fragrant and tender, about 10 minutes. Do not let the garlic brown. Stir in the tomato paste and 1½ teaspoons salt and cook, stirring, for 2 minutes. Pour in the wine and stir to combine. Transfer the contents of the pan to a slow cooker.

Cut off the stem and feathery tops and any bruised outer stalks from the fennel bulb; coarsely chop the feathery tops to yield 2 tablespoons and set aside. Cut the bulb lengthwise into wedges and trim away the core, leaving a little core intact to hold each wedge together. Add the fennel wedges, tomatoes, and stock to the slow cooker, cover, and cook on the low setting for 3 hours. Add the fish, re-cover, and cook for 30 minutes more. The fish should be firm but tender.

Using a slotted spoon, transfer the fish and fennel wedges to a large plate. Remove and discard the bay leaves. Purée the soup with an immersion blender. (Alternatively, for a chunkier soup, transfer half of the mixture to a blender, process until smooth, then return the purée to the slow cooker and stir to combine.)

Ladle the tomato broth into warm shallow bowls, and divide the fish and fennel wedges evenly among the bowls. Garnish each serving with a little orange zest, the reserved chopped fennel tops, and the chervil, if using. Serve at once with the crostini alongside.

Here is an easy version of bouillabaisse, the famed fish soup of Marseilles, crowned with fresh herbs, orange zest, and crunchy crostini. For an even more sublime flavor, substitute 2 tablespoons Pernod or other anise-flavored liqueur for 2 tablespoons of the white wine. For an authentic touch, top the crostini with a dollop of red pepper aioli (page 93).

Salmon with Spring Vegetables

1 cup (8 fl oz/250 ml)
dry white wine

½ cup (4 fl oz/125 ml)
vegetable stock, homemade
(page 215) or purchased

½ small yellow onion, sliced

3 sprigs fresh tarragon

Salt and freshly ground pepper

4 salmon fillets, about
6 oz (185 g) each

1 bunch asparagus,
about 1 lb (500 g)

1 tablespoon unsalted butter

1 tablespoon olive oil

2 leeks, including the light
green tops, cut into 2-inch
(5-cm) matchsticks

2 cups (10 oz/315 g) fresh or
thawed, frozen English peas

Grated zest and juice
of ½ lemon

Snipped fresh chives
for garnish

MAKES 4 SERVINGS

In a slow cooker, stir together ½ cup (4 fl oz/125 ml) water, the wine, stock, onion, tarragon sprigs, ½ teaspoon salt, and several grinds of pepper. Cover and cook on the low setting for 30 minutes. Add the salmon fillets (they can overlap), re-cover, and cook for 1 hour. The fish should be opaque throughout, firm, and very tender.

About 15 minutes before the fish is ready, remove the tough ends from the asparagus spears. Using a vegetable peeler, peel the lower 2 inches (5 cm) of each spear, then cut the spears into 2-inch lengths. Bring a saucepan three-fourths full of salted water to a boil over high heat. Add all the asparagus pieces except the tips and cook for 4 minutes. Add the tips and cook until all the pieces are just tender, about 2 minutes longer. Drain and run under cold running water until cool. Spread the asparagus on a kitchen towel to dry.

In a large frying pan over medium heat, melt the butter with the oil. Add the leeks and sauté for 2 minutes. Add the peas and cook for 1 minute, then add the asparagus and sauté until heated through, 1–2 minutes more. Stir in the lemon juice and remove from the heat.

Transfer the salmon to warm individual plates. Discard the braising liquid. Arrange the vegetables alongside the salmon and scatter the lemon zest and chives over the top. Serve at once.

Here, spring vegetables—asparagus, peas, and leeks—are sautéed in butter and oil just until tender, adding color and garden-fresh flavor to moist, braised salmon. If leeks are unavailable, substitute 12 green onions, including the light green tops, halved lengthwise and then cut crosswise. If desired, serve with steamed red potatoes or creamy mashed potatoes.

Spanish-Style Cod with Peppers

Large pinch of saffron threads

¼ cup (2 fl oz/60 ml) plus 3 tablespoons dry white wine

6 tablespoons (3 fl oz/90 ml) olive oil

20 cloves garlic, peeled but left whole

3 bay leaves

3 plum tomatoes, seeded and coarsely chopped

½ cup (4 fl oz/125 ml) vegetable stock, homemade (page 215) or purchased

Salt and freshly ground pepper

1½ lb (750 g) cod fillets

1 orange

1 small red bell pepper, seeded and finely diced

3 tablespoons coarsely chopped fresh flat-leaf parsley

1½ tablespoons sherry vinegar

MAKES 6 SERVINGS

Soak the saffron in the 3 tablespoons white wine for 20 minutes. In a large, heavy frying pan over low heat, warm 2 tablespoons of the oil. Add the garlic cloves and cook gently, stirring occasionally, until fragrant and tender but not browned, about 10 minutes. Add the remaining ¼ cup wine, then transfer the contents of the pan to a slow cooker.

Stir in the bay leaves, tomatoes, the saffron mixture, the stock, and ¼ teaspoon salt. Cover and cook on the low setting for 3 hours. Stir the liquid, add the fish, re-cover, and continue cooking for 30 minutes more. The fish should be firm yet very tender.

While the fish is cooking, grate the zest from the orange and set aside. Then, trim away the remaining rind and pith and segment the orange as directed on page 217. Roughly chop the segments. In a bowl, combine the orange zest, diced orange segments, bell pepper, parsley, vinegar, and the remaining 4 tablespoons (2 fl oz/60 ml) oil. Season with ¼ teaspoon salt and several grinds of pepper, and stir gently to combine.

Transfer the fish to a warm serving platter or individual plates, dividing it evenly. Remove and discard the bay leaves from the braising liquid. Spoon the orange and pepper mixture over the fish, and then spoon the braised tomatoes and some of the liquid around the fish. Serve at once.

In this dish, whole garlic cloves become tender and mild even though they spend a relatively short time in the slow cooker. If you cannot find cod, substitute another meaty white fish such as tilapia or red snapper. Serve the fish and the luscious, sweet garlic over steamed rice or couscous, with plenty of the colorful, fragrant braising juices.

Olive Oil–Braised Tuna with Tapenade

¼ cup (2 fl oz/60 ml) fish or vegetable stock, homemade (page 215) or purchased

5 tablespoons (3 fl oz/80 ml) extra-virgin olive oil, plus more for drizzling

¼ cup (2 fl oz/60 ml) dry white wine or rosé

½ yellow onion, finely chopped

3 bay leaves

Salt and freshly ground pepper

1½ lb (750 g) tuna fillets or steaks, cut into 4 equal pieces

1 cup (5 oz/155 g) *each* pitted mild green olives such as Picholine or Lucques and black olives such as Niçoise

2 cloves garlic, chopped

1 teaspoon red or white wine vinegar

Grated zest of 1 orange

4 cups (4 oz/125 g) baby spinach

MAKES 4 SERVINGS

In a slow cooker, stir together the stock, 4 tablespoons (2 fl oz/60 ml) of the oil, the wine, onion, bay leaves, ½ teaspoon salt, and several grinds of pepper. Cover and cook on the low setting for 30 minutes to blend the flavors. Add the tuna, re-cover, and cook for 15–20 minutes. The tuna should be firm and opaque throughout.

To make the orange-olive tapenade, in a food processor, combine the green and black olives, the garlic, the remaining 1 tablespoon oil, the vinegar, and orange zest. Pulse to form a chunky tapenade.

In a bowl, drizzle the spinach with a little oil, season with salt and pepper, and toss to coat evenly. Divide the spinach among individual plates, and then divide the tuna among the plates, arranging it on top of the spinach. Top each tuna portion with a spoonful of the tapenade and serve.

While tuna is one of the leanest types of fish and thereby among the fastest cooking, gentle cooking in a slow cooker keeps the fish moist and full of flavor. The firm, meaty flesh is ideal for bold flavors, such as this garlic-laden tapenade of briny olives and tangy orange zest.

VEGETABLES

Each season offers new flavors for the slow cooker. Summer brings ratatouille thick with zucchini, tomatoes, and peppers, and autumn inspires hearty stuffed cabbages and citrus-scented beets. Butternut squash soup and honey-laced sweet potatoes sustain us through the cold months, until spring welcomes crisp, tender peas, green artichokes, and tiny new potatoes.

Spicy Fennel with Olives & Orange

2 fennel bulbs, about 1 lb (500 g) total weight

1 tablespoon extra-virgin olive oil, plus more for drizzling

1 large shallot, minced

4 cloves garlic, minced

¼–½ teaspoon red pepper flakes

2 tablespoons dry white wine

½ teaspoon white wine vinegar

⅓ cup (3 fl oz/80 ml) chicken stock, homemade (page 214) or purchased

2 sprigs fresh oregano, or ½ teaspoon dried oregano

Salt and freshly ground pepper

1 orange

½ cup (2½ oz/75 g) pitted black olives such as Kalamatas or Niçoise, halved

MAKES 4 SERVINGS

Cut off the stem and feathery tops and any bruised outer stalks from each fennel bulb. Chop the feathery tops to yield 2 tablespoons and set aside. Quarter each bulb lengthwise, then halve each quarter lengthwise and trim away the core, leaving a little core intact to hold each wedge together. You should have 16 wedges. Place the fennel in a slow cooker.

In a small, heavy frying pan over medium-high heat, warm the oil. Add the shallot and sauté until lightly golden, about 4 minutes. Add the garlic and pepper flakes to taste and cook for 1 minute more. Pour in the wine and vinegar and stir to dislodge any browned bits on the pan bottom. Stir in the stock, oregano sprigs, ½ teaspoon salt, and several grinds of pepper. Transfer the contents of the pan to the slow cooker. Cover and cook on the low setting for 2½ hours. The fennel should be tender but not mushy.

Just before the fennel is ready, grate the zest from the orange and set aside. Then, trim away the remaining rind and segment the orange as directed on page 217. Coarsely chop the orange segments.

Using a slotted spoon, transfer the fennel wedges to a warm platter. Taste the braising liquid and adjust the seasoning with salt, pepper, and a little more vinegar, if needed. Spoon some of the liquid over the fennel (discard the remainder) and scatter the fennel tops, olives, grated orange zest, and orange segments over the top. Drizzle with olive oil and serve.

Fresh fennel is popular in Italian kitchens, where it appears in braises and soups, on pizzas, and raw in salads. In this dish, it is braised with garlic and then combined with diced orange, which adds a sweet, sunny note. Red pepper flakes impart a little spicy heat, black olives contribute an earthy-salty flavor, and the anise-flavored fennel tops add freshness.

Braised Beets with Arugula & Ricotta Salata

Grated zest of 1 orange

½ cup (4 fl oz/125 ml) fresh orange juice

3 tablespoons rice vinegar

2 sprigs fresh thyme, or 1 teaspoon dried thyme

Salt and freshly ground pepper

3 lb (1.5 kg) orange, yellow, or red beets, peeled and sliced ⅓ inch (9 mm) thick

4 cups (4 oz/125 g) baby arugula

1 shallot, minced

⅓ cup (3 fl oz/80 ml) Orange Vinaigrette (page 216)

¼ lb (125 g) ricotta salata cheese

MAKES 6 SERVINGS

In a slow cooker, stir together the orange zest and juice, vinegar, thyme sprigs, ¼ teaspoon salt, and several grinds of pepper. Add the beets and stir to coat them with the liquid. Cover and cook on the low setting for 4 hours, stirring once or twice, if possible, to redistribute the liquid. The beets should be tender but not falling apart.

Using a slotted spoon, transfer the beets to a serving platter. Discard the braising liquid. In a bowl, combine the arugula and shallot and toss with enough vinaigrette to coat lightly. Arrange the arugula over the beets. Using a vegetable peeler, shave the ricotta salata over the top. Serve at once.

Slow cooking beets brings out their natural sweetness, which is heightened by the addition of orange juice and zest in this recipe. Topping the tender, cooked beets with peppery arugula and a scattering of salty ricotta salata delivers a robust contrast to the sweetness. Serve with grilled chicken or pork chops for the perfect light, summer meal.

Spaghetti with Fresh Tomato-Herb Sauce

1 tablespoon unsalted butter

4 tablespoons (2 fl oz/60 ml) olive oil

1 large yellow onion, finely chopped

3 stalks celery, finely chopped

4 cloves garlic, smashed

1 teaspoon dried oregano

2 tablespoons dry white wine

2 teaspoons red wine vinegar

8 large, ripe tomatoes, about 3½ lb (1.75 kg) total weight, halved crosswise and seeded

Salt and freshly ground pepper

1½ lb (750 g) dried spaghetti or other strand pasta

2 tablespoons coarsely chopped fresh basil

Small handful of coarsely chopped fresh flat-leaf parsley

Grated Parmesan cheese for serving

MAKES 6–8 SERVINGS

In a large, heavy frying pan over medium-high heat, melt the butter with 1 tablespoon of the oil. Add the onion and celery and sauté until lightly golden, about 6 minutes. Add the garlic and oregano and cook for 1 minute more. Pour in the wine and vinegar and stir to dislodge any browned bits on the pan bottom. Transfer the contents of the pan to a slow cooker. Stir in the tomatoes, ½ teaspoon salt, and several grinds of pepper. Cover and cook on the low setting for 4–5 hours, stirring once or twice if possible. The sauce should be thick and flavorful.

Let the sauce cool slightly, then transfer about one-fourth of it to a blender or food processor and process until smooth. Return the purée to the cooker and stir to combine. (Alternatively, use an immersion blender to purée the sauce to the desired consistency.) Cover and keep the sauce warm on the low setting while you cook the pasta.

Bring a large pot three-fourths full of salted water to a boil over high heat. Add the spaghetti, stir well, and cook until al dente, according to package directions. Drain and transfer to a large warm platter or shallow serving bowl. Add the remaining 3 tablespoons olive oil and toss to coat evenly. Add half of the tomato sauce and half each of the basil and parsley and toss again. Spoon the remaining sauce over the top, and scatter with the remaining herbs. Garnish with grated Parmesan and serve at once.

The low, gentle heat of the slow cooker leaves more of the vine-ripened tomato flavor intact in this classic sauce than the traditional stove-top version, yielding a fresher-tasting result. If you have a bumper crop of tomatoes in your garden, double the recipe and freeze it for future use.

Winter Vegetable Stew

4 tablespoons (2 fl oz/60 ml) olive oil

1 large yellow onion, finely chopped

2 stalks celery, finely chopped

10 cloves garlic, smashed

2 tablespoons tomato paste

½ cup (4 fl oz/125 ml) medium-dry sherry

½ cup (4 fl oz/125 ml) chicken or vegetable stock, homemade (page 214–215) or purchased

1 teaspoon sherry vinegar or red wine vinegar

1 butternut squash, about 2½ lb (1.25 kg)

3 parsnips

3 large carrots

1 teaspoon dried tarragon

Salt and freshly ground pepper

Grated zest and juice of 1 lemon

1 bunch watercress, tough stems removed and leaves chopped

MAKES 6 SERVINGS

In a large, heavy frying pan over medium-high heat, warm 2 tablespoons of the oil. Add the onion and celery and sauté until softened and beginning to brown, about 6 minutes. Add the garlic and tomato paste and stir for 1 minute. Pour in the sherry, stock, and vinegar and stir to dislodge any browned bits on the pan bottom. Transfer the contents of the frying pan to a slow cooker.

Peel and seed the butternut squash and cut into chunks. Peel the parsnips and carrots and cut into chunks. Add the butternut squash, parsnips, carrots, and tarragon to the slow cooker, season with salt and pepper, and stir to blend evenly. Cover and cook on the low setting for 5 hours. The vegetables should be tender.

Stir the lemon juice into the stew to taste, then transfer the stew to a warm serving bowl or shallow individual bowls. Drizzle with the remaining olive oil, top with the watercress and a sprinkle of lemon zest, and serve.

This classic cool-weather dish sparkles with color and appealing flavors. Adding the lemon zest to the warm vegetables releases its citrusy, fresh aroma, providing a fresh dimension for a traditionally hearty dish. Accompany with a green salad and crusty country bread.

Braised Fennel with Tarragon

2 large fennel bulbs, about 1 lb (500 g) total weight

1 large shallot, finely chopped

4 cloves garlic, finely chopped

3 sprigs fresh tarragon, plus 1½ teaspoons finely chopped tarragon

Grated zest and juice of 1 large orange

2 tablespoons chicken stock, homemade (page 214) or purchased

Salt and freshly ground pepper

3-oz (90-g) piece dry jack or Parmesan cheese

MAKES 4–6 SERVINGS

Cut off the stem and feathery tops and any bruised outer stalks from each fennel bulb. Coarsely chop the feathery tops to yield 2 tablespoons and set aside. Quarter each bulb lengthwise, then halve each quarter lengthwise and trim away the core, leaving a little core intact to hold each wedge together. You should have 16 thin wedges. Place the fennel in a slow cooker. Add the shallot, garlic, tarragon sprigs, orange juice, stock, ½ teaspoon salt, and several grinds of pepper and stir together gently to avoid breaking up the fennel. Cover and cook on the low setting for 2½ hours. The fennel should be tender but not mushy.

Using a slotted spoon, transfer the fennel wedges to a warm platter. Taste the braising liquid and adjust the seasoning with salt and pepper. Spoon some of the braising liquid over the fennel (discard the remainder), and scatter the orange zest, fennel tops, and chopped tarragon over the top. Using a vegetable peeler, shave the cheese over the top. Serve at once.

In this recipe, fennel is given a French accent with the addition of fresh tarragon. Both fennel and tarragon complement fish beautifully, making this dish a good choice to serve alongside simple grilled or poached sea bass or other meaty white fish.

Sweet-and-Sour Red Cabbage

1 small head red cabbage, halved, cored, and shredded

⅓ cup (4 oz/125 g) honey, warmed until free-flowing

½ cup (4 fl oz/125 ml) sherry vinegar

3 whole cloves

Salt

1 tablespoon unsalted butter

1 tablespoon canola oil

3 Granny Smith or other tart green apples, peeled, cored, and coarsely chopped

Sour cream for serving

2 tablespoons coarsely chopped fresh dill

MAKES 6 SERVINGS

In a slow cooker, stir together the cabbage, honey, vinegar, cloves, and ¼ teaspoon salt. Cover and cook on the low setting for 4 hours, stirring halfway through, if possible. The cabbage should be tender.

Just before the cabbage is ready, in a frying pan over medium-high heat, melt the butter with the oil. Add the apples and cook, stirring occasionally, until beginning brown, about 8 minutes. Add 2 tablespoons water, cover, reduce the heat to low, and cook until the apples have softened but are not mushy, about 5 minutes.

Fold the apples into the cabbage, mixing well. Divide among warm individual plates, top each serving with a dollop of sour cream, and sprinkle with dill. Serve at once.

Cabbage develops a tender, yet not overly soft texture in a slow cooker. Here, it cooks along with honey and sherry vinegar in a perfect balance of sweet and pungent flavors, and then is mixed with tart-sweet browned apples just before serving. If you have apple juice on hand, substitute it for the water when cooking the apples. Serve alongside grilled sausages or pork.

Butternut Squash & Apple Soup

1 butternut squash, about 2½ lb (1.25 kg)

Salt and freshly ground pepper

¼ cup (2 fl oz/60 ml) canola oil

½ small yellow onion, thinly sliced

1 cup (8 fl oz/250 ml) apple juice, preferably unfiltered

1 cup (8 fl oz/250 ml) floral white wine such as Riesling

1 cup (8 fl oz/250 ml) vegetable or chicken stock, homemade (page 214–215) or purchased

1 Granny Smith or other tart green apple, peeled, cored, and cut into small chunks

½ cup (4 fl oz/125 ml) heavy cream

½ cup (4 oz/125 g) plain yogurt

½ teaspoon curry powder

2 tablespoons coarsely chopped fresh flat-leaf parsley

Fried Shallots for garnish (see note; optional)

MAKES 4–6 SERVINGS

Halve the squash lengthwise, scoop out and discard the seeds and strings, and then peel the halves. Cut into 1½-inch (4-cm) chunks and season generously with salt and pepper. In a large, heavy frying pan over medium-high heat, warm the oil. When the oil is hot, working in batches if necessary to avoid crowding, add the squash and sauté until nicely browned, 8–10 minutes. Transfer to a slow cooker.

Add the onion to the frying pan and sauté over medium-high heat until beginning to color, about 5 minutes. Pour in the apple juice and stir to dislodge any browned bits on the pan bottom. Stir in the wine and stock and transfer the contents of the pan to the slow cooker. Cover and cook on the low setting for 3 hours. Add the apple, re-cover, and cook for 1 hour more. The squash and apple should be tender.

Let the soup cool slightly. Working in batches, transfer to a blender and process until smooth. Return the purée to the slow cooker and stir in the cream. Cover and keep warm on the low setting until ready to serve.

In a small bowl, whisk together the yogurt, curry powder, and ¼ teaspoon salt. Ladle the soup into warm shallow bowls and drizzle each serving with some of the curried yogurt. Sprinkle with parsley and scatter the fried shallots, if using, over the top. Serve at once.

ADD CRUNCH WITH **FRIED SHALLOTS** Pour canola oil to a depth of 1 inch (2.5 cm) into a large, deep frying pan and heat to 350°F (180°C) on a deep-frying thermometer. Meanwhile, slice 2 shallots paper-thin and separate into rings. Coat the rings with flour, tapping off the excess. When the oil is ready, add the shallot rings and fry until crisp and golden, about 2 minutes. Using a wire skimmer, transfer to paper towels to drain. Season with salt and freshly ground pepper.

Peperonata

3 tablespoons tomato paste

3 tablespoons plus
2 teaspoons olive oil

1 teaspoon dried oregano

Salt and freshly ground pepper

15 cloves garlic, smashed, plus
2 cloves, finely chopped

1 large onion, halved through
the stem end and thinly sliced

1 sprig fresh rosemary

1 green, 1 yellow, and 2 red
bell peppers, seeded and cut
lengthwise into thin strips

2 tablespoons coarsely
chopped fresh flat-leaf
parsley, plus more for garnish

1 tablespoon red wine vinegar

3 oz (90 g) crumbled feta
for serving

Crostini (page 216) for
serving (optional)

MAKES 4–6 SERVINGS

In a slow cooker, whisk together the tomato paste, the 3 tablespoons oil, the oregano, 1 teaspoon salt, and several grinds of pepper. Add the smashed garlic cloves, onion, rosemary sprig, and bell peppers and mix well. Cover and cook on the low setting for 5 hours, stirring two or three times if possible. The peppers should be tender.

Remove and discard the rosemary sprig. Transfer the contents of the slow cooker to a warm platter or serving bowl.

In a small bowl, whisk together the chopped garlic, the 2 tablespoons parsley, the vinegar, and the remaining 2 teaspoons oil.

Drizzle the garlic-parsley mixture over the pepper mixture, garnish with additional parsley and crumbled feta, and serve at once. If desired, serve the peperonata atop the crostini.

The stunning colors and rich flavor of this popular Italian dish make it an ideal partner for a grilled main course, such as juicy steak or pork tenderloin. Start cooking the peppers in the morning, and then fire up the grill later in the day to quickly cook the rest of the meal. A simple dressing drizzled on top before serving revives this dish's piquant flavors.

Braised Carrots with Couscous

2 lb (1 kg) carrots

1 fennel bulb

5 large cloves garlic, thinly sliced

2 tablespoons olive oil, plus more for drizzling

2 tablespoons white wine vinegar

1 cup (8 fl oz/250 ml) plus 2 tablespoons chicken or vegetable stock, homemade (page 214–215) or purchased

Salt and freshly ground pepper

1 cup (6 oz/185 g) instant couscous

¼ lb (125 g) fresh goat cheese, crumbled (optional)

2–3 tablespoons coarsely chopped fresh dill

Juice of ½ lemon

MAKES 4–6 SERVINGS

Peel the carrots, halve lengthwise, and cut crosswise into chunks about 1 inch (2.5 cm) thick. Cut off the stem and feathery tops and any bruised outer stalks from the fennel bulb. Quarter the bulb lengthwise and trim away the core. Finely chop the fennel bulb.

In a slow cooker, stir together the carrot chunks, chopped fennel, garlic, oil, vinegar, the 2 tablespoons stock, ½ teaspoon salt, and several grinds of pepper. Cover and cook on the low setting for 5 hours. The carrots should be tender.

Just before the carrots are ready, in a small saucepan, bring the remaining 1 cup stock and ¼ teaspoon salt to a boil in a small saucepan. Put the couscous in a heatproof bowl and stir in the hot stock. Cover the bowl and let stand until the liquid is absorbed, about 5 minutes.

Fluff the couscous with a fork and mound on a warm platter. Spoon the carrots and their braising liquid over the top. Scatter the goat cheese (if using) and dill over the carrots, and then drizzle with a little oil and the lemon juice. Serve at once.

Carrots hold their shape beautifully in the gentle heat of a slow cooker. Here, their natural, mildly sweet flavor, which deepens during the extended cooking, is nicely offset by the cool tang of goat cheese and the unique aroma of fresh dill. The carrots and their braising liquid are served over couscous, a tender semolina pasta that readily absorbs the complex liquid.

Garlicky Leeks with Linguine

6 leeks, about 1 inch (2.5 cm) in diameter

8 cloves garlic, peeled but left whole

½ small yellow onion, chopped

½ cup (4 fl oz/125 ml) dry white wine

½ cup (4 fl oz/125 ml) chicken stock, homemade (page 214) or purchased

3 tablespoons olive oil

2 tablespoons white wine vinegar

3 sprigs fresh flat-leaf parsley

3 bay leaves

Salt and freshly ground pepper

12 oz (375 g) fresh linguine or 1 lb (500 g) dried linguine

2 large shallots, minced

3 oz (90 g) thinly sliced prosciutto, cut into narrow strips

3 tablespoons slivered fresh basil leaves

MAKES 4–6 SERVINGS

Trim off the root end and then cut off the dark green tops from each leek, leaving about 2 inches (5 cm) of light green tops attached. Halve the leeks lengthwise, rinse well, then cut crosswise into slices about ¾ inch (2 cm) thick. Transfer to a slow cooker.

Stir in the garlic, onion, wine, stock, 2 tablespoons of the oil, the vinegar, parsley sprigs, bay leaves, ½ teaspoon salt, and several grinds of pepper. Cover and cook on the low setting for 3 hours, stirring once halfway through if possible. The leeks should be very tender. Remove and discard the bay leaves and parsley sprigs. Keep warm.

Bring a large pot three-fourths full of salted water to a boil. Add the linguine, stir well, and cook until al dente, according to package directions. Meanwhile, in a large frying pan over medium heat, warm the remaining 1 tablespoon oil. Add the shallots and prosciutto and sauté until barely softened, about 2 minutes.

When the pasta is ready, drain and add to the frying pan. Add the leeks, including a little of their braising liquid (discard the remainder), and toss over medium heat for a minute or so to mix well. Transfer to a warm platter or individual plates, garnish with the basil, and serve at once.

In this light and elegant pasta, leeks take a star turn. The vinegar adds a tangy note that is often welcome in slow-braised recipes. Prosciutto delivers the rich flavor of cured pork and the basil a bright, herbal taste to the finished dish. Accompany with a salad of mixed greens, sliced pears, crumbled blue cheese, and toasted walnuts.

Spring Vegetable Ragout

6 oz (185 g) new potatoes
or small red potatoes

3 leeks

1 lb (500 g) fresh baby
artichokes, trimmed (page
217) and halved lengthwise or
1 package (14 oz/440 g) frozen
artichoke hearts, thawed and
halved lengthwise

1 cup (6 oz/185 g) cherry or
grape tomatoes, halved

10 cloves garlic, smashed

½ yellow onion, finely chopped

¼ cup (2 fl oz/60 ml)
dry white wine

¼ cup (2 fl oz/60 ml) vegetable
or chicken stock, homemade
(page 214–215) or purchased

2 tablespoons olive oil

4 teaspoons white
wine vinegar

2 sprigs fresh thyme

Salt and freshly ground pepper

4 thin slices pancetta

1½ cups (7½ oz/235 g) fresh
or thawed, frozen English peas

1 tablespoon *each* chopped
fresh mint and fresh basil

MAKES 4–6 SERVINGS

Quarter or halve the potatoes; each piece should be about 1 inch (2.5 cm). Trim the dark green tops from the leeks. Halve the leeks lengthwise, rinse well then cut crosswise about ¼ inch (6 mm) thick. In a slow cooker, combine the leeks, potatoes, the fresh artichoke hearts if using, tomatoes, garlic, onion, wine, stock, oil, vinegar, thyme sprigs, ½ teaspoon salt, and several grinds of pepper and stir to mix well. Cover and cook on the low setting for 3 hours. If using frozen artichoke hearts, add them to the slow cooker after 2 hours of cooking, and stir well.

Meanwhile, preheat the oven to 300°F (150°C). Line a rimmed baking sheet with parchment paper. Place the pancetta slices in a single layer on the prepared pan and cover with a second sheet of parchment. Top with a second baking sheet of the same size. Bake until the pancetta is golden and crisp, 45–50 minutes. Transfer the pancetta to paper towels to drain.

About 5 minutes before the ragout is ready, add the peas, re-cover, and cook until heated through. When the ragout is ready, remove and discard the thyme sprigs. Stir in the mint and basil. Transfer the vegetables and some of their juices to a warm serving bowl or individual plates. Crumble the pancetta into large pieces and scatter over the top. Serve at once.

This bright green, seasonal dish is the perfect way to use spring's bounty of vegetables. Instead of the oven-baked pancetta, you can use crisp crumbled bacon. If you have very tiny potatoes or tomatoes, you can leave them whole. Serve alongside roast chicken or baked ham.

Sweet Potatoes with Honey & Lime

2 lb (1 kg) sweet potatoes

3 tablespoons honey, warmed until free-flowing, plus more for drizzling (optional)

½ teaspoon white wine vinegar

½ teaspoon ground cumin

½ teaspoon ground cinnamon

Grated zest and juice of 1 lime

½ cup (4 fl oz/125 ml) apple juice, preferably unfiltered, or water

Salt and freshly ground pepper

2 tablespoons coarsely chopped fresh cilantro

MAKES 4–6 SERVINGS

Peel the sweet potatoes and cut into 1-inch (2.5-cm) chunks. In a slow cooker, combine the sweet potatoes, honey, vinegar, cumin, cinnamon, lime zest and juice, apple juice, ¼ teaspoon salt, and several grinds of pepper and stir to mix well. Cover and cook on the low setting for about 4½ hours, stirring once or twice if possible. The sweet potatoes should be very tender.

Transfer to a warm serving dish. If desired, drizzle a little more honey over the sweet potatoes. Scatter the cilantro over the top. Serve at once.

Sweet potatoes are a natural for slow cooking which renders them sweet and tender. Lime zest and juice helps cut their natural sweetness, and a shower of chopped cilantro just before serving delivers a fresh, pungent flavor. Serve with roast turkey, chicken, or pork loin.

Cauliflower with Lemon & Mint

3 tablespoons olive oil

1 large head cauliflower, about 1¼ lb (625 g), trimmed and cut into large florets

1 small yellow onion, finely chopped

2 stalks celery, finely chopped

1 teaspoon dried oregano

3 bay leaves

Salt and freshly ground pepper

⅓ cup (3 fl oz/80 ml) vegetable or chicken stock, homemade (page 214–215) or purchased

2 tablespoons fresh lemon juice

Tomato-Olive Relish for serving (see note; optional)

1 tablespoon coarsely chopped fresh mint

Grated zest of ½ lemon

MAKES 4–6 SERVINGS

In a large, heavy frying pan over medium-high heat, warm the oil. When the oil is hot, working in batches if necessary to avoid crowding, add the cauliflower florets and sauté just until beginning to color, about 7 minutes. Using a slotted spoon, transfer to a slow cooker.

Add the onion, celery, oregano, bay leaves, and ½ teaspoon salt to the frying pan and sauté over medium-high heat until the vegetables are softened and lightly colored, 5–6 minutes. Pour in the stock and lemon juice and stir to dislodge any browned bits on the pan bottom. Transfer the contents of the pan to the slow cooker and stir to mix. Cover and cook on the low setting for 2 hours. The cauliflower should be tender.

Remove and discard the bay leaves. Using a slotted spoon, transfer the cauliflower and braising vegetables to a warm serving bowl. Discard the braising liquid. Spoon the tomato relish over the top, if using. Garnish with the mint and lemon zest. Serve at once.

ADD FLAVOR WITH **TOMATO-OLIVE RELISH** In a bowl, whisk together 3 tablespoons extra-virgin olive oil, 1 tablespoon white wine vinegar, ¼ teaspoon salt, and a few grinds of pepper. Fold in ⅔ cup (3½ oz/105 g) green olives, pitted and chopped; 1 ripe tomato, seeded and diced; 1 tablespoon chopped fresh mint; and the grated zest of ½ lemon.

Balsamic-Braised Onions

1 lb (500 g) cipolline onions

1 cinnamon stick

1 cup (8 fl oz/250 ml) chicken or vegetable stock, homemade (page 214–215) or purchased

⅓ cup (3 fl oz/80 ml) balsamic vinegar

1 can (15 oz/470 g) diced tomatoes, drained

Salt and freshly ground pepper

1 teaspoon finely chopped fresh sage

Goat Cheese Bruschetta for serving (see note; optional)

MAKES 8 SERVINGS

Bring a saucepan three-fourths full of water to a boil. Add the onions and boil for 1 minute. Drain in a colander and place under cold running water until cool. Trim a thin slice off the root and stem ends of each onion, keeping a little of the root end intact to help them stay together during cooking. Peel the onions, then cut each in half lengthwise.

In a slow cooker, combine the onions, cinnamon stick, stock, vinegar, tomatoes, ½ teaspoon salt, and several grinds of pepper and stir to mix well. Cover and cook on the low setting for 6 hours. The onions should be tender and just beginning to fall apart.

Using a slotted spoon, transfer the onions and tomatoes to a warm serving bowl, garnish with the sage, and serve at once. Alternatively, if making the bruschetta, spoon the onions and tomatoes onto the cheese-topped bruschetta, sprinkle with the sage, and serve.

ADD CRUNCH WITH **GOAT CHEESE BRUSCHETTA** Preheat a broiler. Arrange 8 wide slices country bread, about ¾ inch (2 cm) thick, on a baking sheet. Broil, turning once, until golden on both sides, 1–2 minutes total. Remove from the broiler and top the slices with ¾ lb (375 g) fresh goat cheese, at room temperature, spreading a thick layer on each slice.

Carrot-Ginger Soup

1 tablespoon unsalted butter

1 tablespoon olive oil

½ yellow onion, finely chopped

2 lb (1 kg) carrots, peeled and cut into 1-inch (2.5-cm) chunks

3 small parsnips, peeled and cut into 1-inch (2.5-cm) chunks

1 teaspoon light brown sugar

6 cups (48 fl oz/1.5 l) vegetable or chicken stock, homemade (page 214–215) or purchased

¼ cup (1¼ oz/35 g) peeled and finely chopped fresh ginger

Salt and freshly ground pepper

Crispy Leeks for serving (see note; optional)

1 tablespoon chopped fresh flat-leaf parsley (optional)

MAKES 6–8 SERVINGS

In a large, heavy frying pan over medium heat, melt the butter with the oil. Add the onion, carrots, and parsnips and sauté until the onions are softened but not browned, about 6 minutes. Sprinkle with the brown sugar and cook, stirring, for 1 minute more. Pour in 1 cup (8 fl oz/250 ml) of the stock and stir to dislodge any browned bits on the pan bottom. Transfer the contents of the pan to a slow cooker. Stir in the remaining 5 cups (40 fl oz/1.25 l) stock, the ginger, ¾ teaspoon salt, and several grinds of pepper. Cover and cook on the low setting for 4 hours. The carrots should be very tender.

Let the soup cool slightly. Working in batches, transfer the soup to a blender or food processor and process until smooth. Transfer to the slow cooker and re-warm on the low setting.

Ladle the soup into warm shallow bowls. If desired, top each portion with the crispy leeks and sprinkle with parsley. Serve at once.

ADD CRUNCH WITH **CRISPY LEEKS** Cut 2 large leeks, white part only, into fine matchsticks and pat thoroughly dry. Pour canola oil to a depth of 1 inch (2.5 cm) into a large, deep frying pan and heat to 350°F (180°C) on a deep-frying thermometer. Add the leeks and fry until crisp and golden, about 2 minutes. Do not overcook. Using a slotted spoon, transfer to paper towels to drain. Season with salt and pepper and use at once.

Braised Potatoes & Escarole

1 tablespoon unsalted butter

1 tablespoon olive oil

1 lb (500 g) small fingerling or red potatoes, halved lengthwise

1 large yellow onion, halved through the stem end and thinly sliced crosswise

2 sprigs fresh thyme

2/3 cup (5 fl oz/160 ml) chicken stock, homemade (page 214) or purchased

2 teaspoons sherry vinegar

Salt and freshly ground pepper

1 head escarole or curly endive, cored, halved lengthwise, and roughly chopped

1 orange

1/3 cup (3 fl oz/80 ml) Orange Vinaigrette (page 216)

MAKES 4–6 SERVINGS

In a large frying pan over medium-high heat, melt the butter with the oil. When the oil is hot, add the potatoes cut sides down and cook without turning until beginning to brown, 5–7 minutes. Using a slotted spoon, transfer the potatoes to a slow cooker.

Add the onion and thyme sprigs to the frying pan and sauté over medium-high heat until golden, about 5 minutes. Pour in the stock and vinegar and stir to dislodge any browned bits on the pan bottom. Stir in ½ teaspoon salt and several grinds of pepper and pour the contents of the pan into the slow cooker. Cover and cook on the high setting for 1 hour.

Stir in the escarole, re-cover, and cook for 30–45 minutes more. The potatoes and escarole should be tender.

Grate the zest from the orange and use to prepare the orange vinaigrette. Trim away the remaining rind and segment the orange as directed on page 217. Coarsely chop the orange segments. Add the vinaigrette to a large shallow serving bowl. Transfer the braised vegetables and some of their braising juices to the bowl, add the chopped orange segments, and stir gently to mix well. Serve at once.

This versatile dish complements everything from roast chicken and grilled steak to panfried sausages and leg of lamb. The escarole and potatoes, which emerge meltingly tender from the slow cooker, are drizzled with a zesty vinaigrette and diced orange, which together lighten the braised vegetables and sharpen their flavor.

Cherry Tomato Ragù with Polenta

2 tablespoons olive oil

2 large shallots, finely chopped

1 stalk celery, finely chopped

4 cloves garlic, smashed

2 sprigs fresh oregano

2 tablespoons dry white wine

1 teaspoon red wine vinegar

2½ lb (1.25 kg) cherry or grape tomatoes, halved or left whole if small

Salt and freshly ground pepper

2 cups (12 oz/375 g) instant polenta

3 tablespoons coarsely chopped fresh basil leaves

MAKES ABOUT 8 SERVINGS

In a large, heavy frying pan over medium heat, warm the oil. Add the shallots and celery and sauté until lightly golden, about 6 minutes. Add the garlic and oregano sprigs and cook for 1 minute more. Pour in the wine, vinegar, and 2 tablespoons water and stir to dislodge any browned bits on the pan bottom. Transfer the contents of the pan to a slow cooker. Stir in the tomatoes, ½ teaspoon salt, and several grinds of pepper. Cover and cook on the low setting for 3–4 hours, stirring two or three times if possible. The tomatoes should be mostly broken down and the sauce should be juicy. Remove the oregano sprigs.

Just before the sauce is ready, in a saucepan, bring 9 cups (72 fl oz/2.25 l) water and 1 tablespoon salt to a boil over high heat. Reduce the heat to low and add the polenta in a slow, steady stream while whisking constantly. Cook, stirring constantly, until the polenta thickens and starts to pull away from the sides of the pan, about 5 minutes.

Divide the soft polenta among warm shallow bowls, top each portion with a heaping spoonful of the ragù, sprinkle with the basil, and serve at once.

This chunky ragù can also be spooned over grilled fish, chicken, or pork or simply tossed with pasta. The cherry tomatoes collapse in the slow cooker but are still identifiable, which contributes to the rustic charm of the dish. You can also scoop out one-fourth of the sauce, purée it in a food processor, then stir the purée back in, to create a more refined ragù.

Citrusy Leeks with Poached Eggs

6 leeks

8 cloves garlic, thinly sliced

½ small yellow onion, chopped

½ cup (4 fl oz/125 ml) fresh orange juice

½ cup (4 fl oz/125 ml) chicken stock, homemade (page 214) or purchased

3 tablespoons white wine vinegar

2 tablespoons olive oil, plus more for drizzling

Salt and freshly ground pepper

4 large eggs

Sriracha sauce for drizzling (optional)

2 tablespoons finely snipped fresh chives

1 tablespoon coarsely chopped fresh flat-leaf parsley

MAKES 4 SERVINGS

Trim off the root end and then cut off the dark green tops from each leek, leaving about 2 inches (5 cm) of light green tops attached. Halve the leeks lengthwise, rinse well, then cut crosswise into slices about ¾ inch (2 cm) thick. Transfer the leeks to a slow cooker.

Add the garlic, onion, orange juice, stock, 2 tablespoons of the vinegar, the 2 tablespoons oil, ½ teaspoon salt, and several grinds of pepper. Cover and cook on the low setting for 3 hours, stirring once halfway through if possible. The leeks should be very tender. Keep warm.

To poach the eggs, fill a large, deep sauté pan three-fourths full of water, bring to a rolling boil over high heat, and add the remaining 1 tablespoon vinegar. Crack an egg into a small ramekin or bowl. Turn the heat to low and, holding the ramekin just above the surface of the barely simmering water, slip the egg into the water. Repeat with the remaining eggs, working as quickly as possible and keeping the eggs separated in the water. When all the eggs are in the water, cover the pan and leave undisturbed for about 3 minutes if you like the yolks runny, and 5 minutes if you like the yolks set.

Divide the leeks among warm individual plates. Using a slotted spoon, place a poached egg on each bed of leeks. Drizzle the eggs with a little oil and chile sauce, if using, sprinkle with the chives and parsley, and serve.

Topping tender leeks with farm-fresh poached eggs results in a stylish yet rustic dish. Drizzling fiery-hot Sriracha chile sauce on top of each egg complements the entire dish. For a memorable brunch, serve with crisp bacon, warm croissants, and freshly squeezed orange juice.

French Onion Soup

3 tablespoons unsalted butter

4 large yellow onions, thinly sliced

¾ teaspoon sugar

Salt and freshly ground pepper

¼ cup (2 fl oz/60 ml) dry white wine

¼ cup (2 fl oz/60 ml) medium-dry sherry

5 cups (40 fl oz/ 1.25 l) beef stock, homemade (page 214) or purchased

2 sprigs fresh thyme

12 slices baguette

½ cup (2 oz/60 g) grated Parmesan or Gruyère cheese

3 tablespoons finely snipped fresh chives

MAKES 4–6 SERVINGS

In a large, heavy frying pan over medium heat, melt the butter. Stir in the onions, cover, and cook, stirring occasionally, until softened but not browned, about 15 minutes. Stir in the sugar, ½ teaspoon salt, and several grinds of pepper and continue cooking uncovered, stirring frequently, until the onions are golden brown, about 20 minutes more. Transfer the onions to a slow cooker. Pour the white wine and sherry into the pan and stir to dislodge any browned bits on the pan bottom. Transfer the contents of the pan to the slow cooker and stir in the stock and thyme sprigs. Cover and cook on the low setting for 4½–5 hours. The onions should be very soft.

Just before the soup is ready, preheat the broiler. Arrange the baguette slices on a rimmed baking sheet and top them with an even layer of the cheese. Broil until the tops are golden, about 30 seconds.

Remove and discard the thyme sprigs from the soup. Ladle the soup into warm shallow bowls. Top each serving with the cheese toasts and sprinkle with the chives. Serve at once.

This classic soup traditionally requires nearly constant attention—up to an hour of frequent stirring over heat—to develop the flavor of the onions. In this recipe, the onions are cooked on the stove top for only about a half hour, then added to the slow cooker for the balance of the cooking. If you don't have sherry on hand, double the amount of white wine. And if you prefer the classic cheese toasts, substitute Gruyère for the Parmesan.

Beets with Escarole & Goat Cheese

½ cup (4 fl oz/125 ml) apple juice, preferably unfiltered

3 tablespoons rice vinegar

1 thick slice yellow onion

Salt and freshly ground pepper

3 lb (1.5 kg) red or yellow beets (about 8), peeled and quartered

1 head escarole

2 tablespoons olive oil

2 cloves garlic, thinly sliced

1 shallot, thinly sliced

3 oz (90 g) fresh goat cheese, crumbled

MAKES 6–8 SERVINGS

In a slow cooker, combine the apple juice, vinegar, onion, ¼ teaspoon salt, and several grinds of pepper. Add the beets and stir to coat them with the liquid. Cover and cook on the low setting for 4 hours, stirring once or twice if possible to redistribute the liquid. The beets should be tender but not falling apart.

About 20 minutes before the beets are ready, remove any bruised outer leaves and the core from the escarole. Cut the leaves crosswise into roughly 2-inch (5-cm) lengths. In a large frying pan over low heat, warm the oil. Add the garlic and shallot and sauté until softened but not browned, about 6 minutes. Season with salt and pepper, stir in the escarole, and cover the pan. Cook, turning the escarole with tongs every 2–3 minutes, until tender but still bright green, about 10 minutes.

Transfer the escarole to a warm platter. Using a slotted spoon, arrange the beets on top of the escarole. Discard the braising liquid. Scatter the goat cheese over the top and serve at once.

Beets and goat cheese are natural partners, often turning up together in salads. In this warm vegetable side dish, they are joined by escarole, which brings crisp texture and flavor to the combination. If some of the beets are much larger than the others, cut them into eighths instead of quarters, so that the chunks are about the same size (ideally about 2 inches/5 cm).

Stuffed Artichokes

1 lemon, halved

4 globe artichokes

3 tablespoons olive oil

½ yellow onion, finely chopped

1 small bunch Swiss chard, stems removed and finely chopped and leaves thinly sliced

1½ teaspoons minced fresh rosemary

4 cloves garlic, sliced

3 tomatoes, seeded and diced

3 oz (90 g) feta cheese, diced

Salt and freshly ground pepper

½ cup (4 fl oz/125 ml) dry white wine

½ cup (4 fl oz/125 ml) chicken stock, homemade (page 214) or purchased

1 teaspoon white wine vinegar

Garlicky Bread Crumbs for serving (see note; optional)

MAKES 4 SERVINGS

Fill a large bowl three-fourths full of cold water, squeeze in the juice of the lemon, and add the spent lemon halves. Working with 1 artichoke at a time, and using a sharp knife, trim off the base of the stem, and then cut off the top one-third of the artichoke. Pull off and discard the tough, dark green outer leaves. Using scissors, snip off any prickly leaf tips that remain. Using the knife, trim any remnants of the tough, dark leaves from the base of the artichoke, and then peel the stem, removing the tough outer layer. Halve the artichoke lengthwise, and scoop out the pale, hairy choke with a spoon. Drop the artichoke halves into the lemon water to prevent browning. Repeat with the remaining 3 artichokes.

In a large, heavy frying pan over medium heat, warm the oil. Add the onion, chard stems, and rosemary and sauté until starting to soften, about 5 minutes. Add the garlic and chard leaves and stir until the leaves are wilted, 5–7 minutes. Remove from the heat and stir in the tomatoes, feta cheese, ½ teaspoon salt, and several grinds of pepper.

Retrieve the artichoke halves from the lemon water (reserve the water), and place cut side up on a work surface. Mound the filling high in the center of each half, packing it firmly. Place the artichokes, stuffing side up, in a slow cooker. Drizzle the wine, stock, vinegar, and about 1 cup (8 fl oz/250 ml) of the lemon water around the edges to reach to just below the cut surface of the artichokes. Cover and cook on the low setting for 5–6 hours. The artichokes are ready when the bases are tender.

Using a slotted spoon, carefully lift the artichoke halves from the braising liquid and divide evenly among individual plates. Discard the braising liquid. If using, scatter the bread crumbs over the artichokes and serve.

ADD CRUNCH WITH **GARLICKY BREAD CRUMBS** Turn on a food processor, drop 3 cloves garlic through the feed tube, and process until finely chopped, about 10 seconds. Add 3 thick slices country bread, crusts removed and torn into large pieces; ¼ teaspoon salt; and several grinds of pepper. Process until coarse crumbs form. Drizzle in 2 tablespoons extra-virgin olive oil and process until well mixed. Transfer the mixture to a large frying pan over medium heat and cook, stirring, until golden, 2–3 minutes. Remove from the pan and toss with 2 tablespoons chopped fresh flat-leaf parsley.

Summer Ratatouille

1 eggplant, about 1 lb (500 g)

Salt and freshly ground pepper

3 zucchini

2 red bell peppers

3 tablespoons tomato paste

3 tablespoons olive oil, plus more for drizzling

4 cloves garlic, finely chopped

1 teaspoon dried oregano

1 large yellow onion, halved and thinly sliced

4 plum tomatoes, quartered lengthwise and seeded

¼ cup (⅓ oz/10 g) fresh flat-leaf parsley, finely chopped

3 tablespoons coarsely chopped fresh basil leaves

⅓ cup (2½ oz/75 g) capers, rinsed and drained

MAKES 4–6 SERVINGS

Cut the eggplant into chunks about 1-inch (2.5-cm) thick. In a colander, toss the eggplant with 1 teaspoon salt. Let drain for about 30 minutes. Pat dry with paper towels.

Trim the zucchini, then halve lengthwise and cut crosswise into slices about ⅓ inch (9 mm) thick. Trim the bell peppers, remove the seeds and ribs, and cut into strips.

In a small bowl, whisk together the tomato paste, olive oil, garlic, oregano, 1 teaspoon salt, and several grinds of pepper. Arrange about one-fourth each of the eggplant, onion, bell pepper, zucchini, and tomatoes in a layer in the bottom of a slow cooker. Spoon one-fourth of the tomato paste mixture over the top. Repeat to make 3 more layers each of vegetables and tomato paste mixture. Cover and cook on the low setting for 5 hours, stirring two or three times if possible.

Transfer the ratatouille to a serving dish and serve hot, warm, or at room temperature. Just before serving, stir in the parsley, sprinkle with the basil and capers, and drizzle with a little oil.

In southern France, particularly along the Mediterranean coast, ratatouille is ubiquitous on summer menus. It is equally delicious hot, warm, or at room temperature, and tastes even better after a day in the refrigerator. Be sure to return the fragrant vegetable stew to room temperature or warm it before serving. The addition of fresh basil and salty, piquant capers just before serving heightens the flavors of the vegetables.

LEGUMES
& GRAINS

The slow cooker masterfully transforms beans, lentils, and grains, turning these pantry staples into tender dishes filled with flavor. Sit down to creamy polenta studded with fresh, sweet corn and topped with woodsy mushrooms; black bean soup brightened with tangy tomatillos; or a classic risotto punctuated with nutty artichoke hearts and mushrooms.

Braised Chickpeas with Spinach

2½ cups (1 lb/500 g) dried chickpeas, picked over and rinsed

2 tablespoons olive oil

1 large yellow onion, coarsely chopped

1 large carrot, peeled and coarsely chopped

1 stalk celery, finely chopped

3 bay leaves

3 cups (24 fl oz/750 ml) chicken or vegetable stock, homemade (page 214–215) or purchased

Salt and freshly ground pepper

1 can (15 oz/470 g) diced tomatoes, drained

Baby Spinach Salad for serving (see note; optional)

MAKES 6 SERVINGS

In a large bowl, combine the chickpeas with water to cover by 2 inches (5 cm) and let soak overnight. Drain well.

In a large, heavy frying pan over medium heat, warm the oil. Add the onion, carrot, celery, and bay leaves and sauté until softened but not browned, about 6 minutes. Pour in the stock and stir to dislodge any browned bits on the pan bottom. Transfer the contents of the pan to the slow cooker and stir in the chickpeas. Cover and cook on the low setting for 6 hours. Stir in 1 teaspoon salt, several grinds of pepper, and the tomatoes, re-cover, and cook for 2 hours more. The chickpeas should be tender but not mushy.

Remove and discard the bay leaves. Using a slotted spoon, transfer the chickpeas and vegetables to a serving bowl and moisten the chickpeas with some of the braising liquid. Top the chickpeas with the spinach salad, if using. Serve at once.

ADD FRESHNESS WITH **BABY SPINACH SALAD** In a bowl, whisk together ¾ cup (4½ oz/140 g) minced red onion; 2 cloves garlic, minced; 2 tablespoons red wine vinegar; ¼ teaspoon salt; and several grinds of pepper. Whisk in 6 tablespoons (3 fl oz/90 ml) extra-virgin olive oil. Add 2 cups (2 oz/60 g) baby spinach to the bowl and toss to coat evenly.

White Beans with Gremolata

2¼ cups (1 lb/500 g) dried cannellini or other small white beans, picked over and rinsed

6 cloves garlic, smashed, plus 2 tablespoons minced garlic

2 sprigs fresh sage

6 cups (48 fl oz/1.5 l) chicken or vegetable stock, homemade (page 214–215) or purchased

Salt and freshly ground pepper

2 tablespoons grated lemon zest

2 tablespoons finely chopped fresh flat-leaf parsley

2 tablespoons extra-virgin olive oil

MAKES 6 SERVINGS

In a large bowl, combine the beans with water to cover by 2 inches (5 cm) and let soak overnight. Drain well.

Place the drained beans in a slow cooker. Add the garlic cloves, sage sprigs, and stock. The stock should cover the beans by about 2 inches; add water as needed to supplement. Cover and cook on the low setting for 5½–6 hours. The beans should be tender but not falling apart. Stir in 1 teaspoon salt, re-cover, and cook for 30 minutes more.

Remove and discard the sage sprigs. Drain the beans in a colander and discard the braising liquid. Transfer the beans to a serving bowl. Season to taste with pepper and keep warm.

To make the gremolata, in a small bowl, stir together the lemon zest, minced garlic, and parsley. Drizzle the beans with the oil and scatter the gremolata over the top. Serve at once.

Here, gremolata, a mixture of lemon zest, garlic, and parsley traditionally served atop Italian osso buco, tops creamy white beans flavored with sage. Use your best-quality extra-virgin olive oil for drizzling over this dish. Its fruity perfume will be released the moment it hits the warm beans. Serve with roast pork or panfried lamb chops.

Split Pea Soup

1 tablespoon olive oil

1 yellow onion, finely chopped

2 stalks celery, finely chopped

2 tablespoons dry white wine

2¼ cups (1 lb/500 g)
green split peas,
picked over and rinsed

6 cups (48 fl oz/1.5 l)
chicken stock, homemade
(page 214) or purchased

1 smoked ham hock,
about 1½ lb (750 g)

Salt and freshly ground pepper

Fennel-Bacon Salad for
serving (see note; optional)

MAKES 4–6 SERVINGS

In a heavy frying pan over medium heat, warm the oil. Add the onion and celery and sauté until softened, about 5 minutes. Pour in the wine and stir to dislodge any browned bits on the pan bottom. Transfer the contents of the pan to a slow cooker. Add the split peas, stock, and ham hock, cover, and cook on the low setting for 9 hours. The split peas should be very tender.

Remove the ham hock, pull off the meat, and discard the skin, bone, and cartilage. Shred the meat and set aside.

Transfer about one-third of the soup to a blender or food processor and process until smooth. Return the soup to the slow cooker, add the reserved meat, and stir well. Season to taste with salt and pepper. Re-warm the soup on the low setting.

Ladle the soup into warm bowls and top with the fennel-bacon salad, if using. Serve at once.

ADD CRUNCH WITH **FENNEL-BACON SALAD** In a frying pan over medium heat, cook 4–6 thick-cut bacon slices until browned and crisp, about 5 minutes. Drain on paper towels, then crumble. Cut off the stem and feathery tops and any bruised outer parts from 1 small fennel bulb. Coarsely chop the feathery tops to yield 2 tablespoons and set aside. Halve the fennel bulb lengthwise, then core and cut crosswise into paper-thin slices. In a bowl, combine the fennel slices, reserved fennel tops, crumbled bacon, and the grated zest of 1 lemon. Toss to mix well.

White Bean & Cherry Tomato Salad

2¼ cups (1 lb/500 g) dried Great Northern or other small white beans, picked over and rinsed

6 cloves garlic, sliced

2 sprigs fresh flat-leaf parsley

3 bay leaves

6 cups (48 fl oz/1.5 l) chicken or vegetable stock, homemade (page 214–215) or purchased

Salt and freshly ground pepper

⅓–½ cup (3–4 fl oz/80–125 ml) Parsley Vinaigrette (page 216)

2 cups (12 oz/375 g) cherry tomatoes, halved or quartered

2 tablespoons chopped fresh flat-leaf parsley

3-oz (90-g) piece *pecorino romano* cheese

MAKES 6 SERVINGS

In a large bowl, combine the beans with water to cover by 2 inches (5 cm) and let soak overnight. Drain well.

Place the drained beans in a slow cooker. Add the garlic, parsley sprigs, bay leaves, and stock. The stock should cover the beans by about 2 inches; add water as needed to supplement. Cover and cook on the low setting for 5½–6 hours. The beans should be tender but not falling apart. Stir in 1 teaspoon salt, re-cover, and cook for 30 minutes more.

Remove and discard the parsley sprigs and bay leaves. Drain the beans in a colander set over a bowl, reserving the braising liquid. Transfer the beans to a serving bowl and stir in the vinaigrette and tomatoes. Season the beans to taste with salt and pepper. Add a little braising liquid if needed to moisten the beans.

To serve, sprinkle the beans with the chopped parsley. Using a vegetable peeler, shave the pecorino over the top, then serve.

Serve this well-balanced side dish any time sweet, ripe cherry tomatoes are in the market. It is an ideal companion to grilled chicken and zucchini for a warm weather supper, or to garlic-laced spinach and pan-roasted lamb chops for an autumn menu.

Black Bean Soup

2¼ cups (1 lb/500 g) dried black beans, picked over and rinsed

1 lb (500 g) tomatillos, husks removed and halved

1 large yellow onion, finely chopped

2 stalks celery, finely chopped

1 carrot, peeled and finely chopped

½ teaspoon red pepper flakes

5 cups (40 fl oz/1.25 l) chicken stock, homemade (page 214) or purchased

¼ cup (2 fl oz/60 ml) medium-dry sherry

1 teaspoon sherry vinegar

1 smoked ham hock, about ½ lb (750 g)

Salt and freshly ground pepper

Corn-Avocado Salsa for serving (see note; optional)

¾ cup (4 oz/125 g) crumbled *queso fresco* (optional)

MAKES 6–8 SERVINGS

In a large bowl, combine the beans with water to cover by 2 inches (5 cm) and let soak overnight. Drain well.

Preheat the broiler. Arrange the tomatillos on a rimmed baking sheet. Broil, turning as needed, until blackened on all sides, 5–7 minutes total. Transfer the tomatillos to a slow cooker and stir in the drained beans, onion, celery, carrot, pepper flakes, stock, sherry, and vinegar. Add the ham hock. Cover and cook on the low setting for 8–9 hours. The beans should be very tender.

Remove the ham hock, pull off the meat, and discard the skin, bone, and cartilage. Shred the meat and set aside.

In batches if necessary, transfer the contents of the slow cooker to a blender or food processor and process until smooth. Return the soup to the slow cooker, add the reserved meat, and stir well. Season to taste with salt and pepper. Re-warm the soup on the low setting.

Ladle the soup into warm individual shallow bowls and top each serving with a spoonful of the corn-avocado salsa and the crumbled cheese, if using. Serve at once.

ADD FLAVOR WITH **CORN-AVOCADO SALSA** In a small frying pan over medium-high heat, warm 2 teaspoons unsalted butter or extra-virgin olive oil. Add 1½ cups (9 oz/280 g) fresh or thawed, frozen corn kernels and sauté until just beginning to brown, about 5 minutes. In a bowl, toss together the corn; 6 green onions, including the light green tops, finely chopped; 1 avocado, halved, pitted, peeled, and diced; 2 tablespoons chopped fresh cilantro; and the juice of 1 lime. Season with salt and freshly ground pepper.

Herbed Lentil Soup

2 tablespoons olive oil

1 large yellow onion, finely chopped

1 carrot, peeled and finely chopped

2 stalks celery, finely chopped

5 cloves garlic, thinly sliced

1 teaspoon ground cumin

1 teaspoon dried oregano

1 tablespoon tomato paste

½ cup (4 fl oz/125 ml) dry red wine

6 cups (48 fl oz/1.5 l) chicken stock, homemade (page 214) or purchased

2¼ cups (1 lb/500 g) brown lentils, picked over and rinsed

¼ lb (125 g) cooked ham, finely diced

Salt and freshly ground pepper

Goat Cheese Crostini for serving (see note; optional)

1 tablespoon chopped fresh dill

MAKES 6 SERVINGS

In a large, heavy frying pan over medium-high heat, warm the oil. Add the onion, carrot, and celery and sauté until softened and beginning to brown, about 6 minutes. Stir in the garlic, cumin, and oregano and cook for about 1 minute more. Stir in the tomato paste and cook for another minute. Pour in the wine and 1 cup (8 fl oz/250 ml) of the stock and stir to dislodge any browned bits on the pan bottom. Transfer the contents of the pan to a slow cooker. Stir in the remaining 5 cups (40 fl oz/1.25 l) stock, the lentils, the ham, ¼ teaspoon salt, and several grinds of pepper. Cover and cook on the low setting for 5 hours. The lentils should be very tender.

Let the soup cool slightly. Transfer about one-third of the soup to a food processor or blender and process until very smooth, about 30 seconds. Return the purée to the soup and stir well.

Ladle the soup into warm shallow bowls. Gently place a crostini in the center of each serving, if using. Sprinkle the soup with a little pepper, and scatter the dill over the top. Serve at once.

ADD CRUNCH WITH GOAT CHEESE CROSTINI Preheat the oven to 350°F (180°C). Arrange 6 baguette slices, about ½ inch (12 mm) thick, on a rimmed baking sheet and brush lightly with olive oil. Bake, turning once, until golden brown, 10–15 minutes. Slice 1 peeled garlic clove in half lengthwise. Carefully rub each baguette slice on one side with a cut side of the garlic clove while still warm. Top the baguette slices with ¼ lb (125 g) fresh goat cheese, at room temperature, dividing it evenly and spreading each slice with a nice thick layer.

Garlicky Lentils with Ham

1 smoked ham hock, about 1½ lb (750 g)

2½ cups (20 fl oz/625 ml) chicken stock, homemade (page 214) or purchased

½ cup (4 fl oz/125 ml) dry red wine

½ yellow onion, halved through the stem end

1 carrot, peeled and finely chopped

1 stalk celery, cut into 2-inch (5-cm) lengths

20 cloves garlic, peeled but left whole

3 bay leaves

2 sprigs fresh thyme

1 teaspoon ground cumin

1½ cups (10½ oz/330 g) green Puy lentils, picked over and rinsed

Salt and freshly ground pepper

Cucumber-Mint Salad for serving (see note; optional)

MAKES 4–6 SERVINGS

Add the ham hock, stock, wine, onion, carrot, celery, garlic, bay leaves, thyme sprigs, and cumin to a slow cooker and stir to mix well. Cover and cook on the low setting for 3 hours. Stir in the lentils, re-cover, and cook for 1½ hours more. The lentils should be tender but not mushy.

Remove the ham hock, bay leaves, onion and celery pieces, and thyme sprigs. Pull the meat off the ham hock and discard the bone, cartilage, skin, and fat. Shred the meat. Stir the shredded meat back into the lentils. Add several grinds of pepper and salt to taste.

Using a slotted spoon, transfer the lentils to a shallow serving bowl. If using, spoon the cucumber salad over the lentils. Serve at once.

ADD FRESHNESS WITH **CUCUMBER-MINT SALAD** In a bowl, whisk together 1½ tablespoons sherry vinegar, ¼ cup (2 fl oz/60 ml) extra-virgin olive oil, ¼ teaspoon salt, and several grinds of pepper. Add ½ English cucumber, peeled and cut into matchsticks; 4–5 green onions, including the light green tops, finely chopped; and 2–3 tablespoons finely chopped fresh mint. Mix together gently.

Spicy Red Bean & Chorizo Stew

2¼ cups (1 lb/500 g) dried red kidney beans, picked over and rinsed

2 tablespoons canola oil

1 large onion, finely chopped

3 stalks celery, finely chopped

1 green bell pepper, seeded and diced

6 cloves garlic, finely chopped

Salt and freshly ground pepper

4 cups (32 fl oz/1 l) beef or chicken stock, homemade (page 214) or purchased

2 teaspoons red wine vinegar

½–¾ teaspoon red pepper flakes

3 bay leaves

1 lb (500 g) cured Spanish-style chorizo, cut into slices ¼ inch (6 mm) thick

Tabasco or other hot-pepper sauce

Cooked white rice for serving

Jicama Salad for serving (see note; optional)

MAKES 6–8 SERVINGS

In a large bowl, combine the beans with water to cover by 2 inches (5 cm) and let soak overnight. Drain well.

In a large, heavy frying pan over medium-high heat, warm the oil. Add the onion, celery, and bell pepper and sauté until softened and just beginning to brown, about 6 minutes. Add the garlic, season with salt and pepper, and cook for 1 minute more. Pour in 1 cup (8 fl oz/250 ml) of the stock and stir to dislodge any browned bits on the pan bottom. Transfer the contents of the pan to a slow cooker and stir in the drained beans, the remaining 3 cups (24 fl oz/750 ml) stock, the vinegar, pepper flakes to taste, the bay leaves, and chorizo. Cover and cook on the low setting for 6–8 hours, stirring once or twice if possible. The beans should be very tender.

Remove and discard the bay leaves. Season to taste with salt, several grinds of pepper, and Tabasco. If you like, using the back of a spoon, mash some of the beans against the inside of the cooker to thicken the stew.

Divide the rice among warm shallow bowls and ladle the bean stew over the rice. Top each serving with a large spoonful of the jicama salad, if using, and serve at once.

ADD ZING WITH JICAMA SALAD Peel a ¾-lb (375-g) jicama and shred it on the large holes of a box grater or, using a large, sharp knife, cut it into thin slices, and then matchsticks. In a bowl, whisk together ⅓–½ cup (3–4 fl oz/80–125 ml) Lemon Vinaigrette (page 216), 2 tablespoons chopped fresh flat-leaf parsley or cilantro, and 1–2 teaspoons prepared horseradish. Add the jicama and toss to coat evenly.

Italian Pasta & Bean Soup

1½ cups (10½ oz/330 g) dried Great Northern or other small white beans

2 tablespoons olive oil

1 yellow onion, finely chopped

2 carrots, peeled and finely chopped

2 stalks celery, finely chopped

5 cloves garlic, finely chopped

1 teaspoon dried oregano

5 cups (40 fl oz/1.25 l) chicken stock, homemade (page 214) or purchased

1 can (15 oz/470 g) diced tomatoes, drained

3-inch (7.5-cm) piece Parmesan cheese rind (optional)

¾ cup (3 oz/90 g) tubetti or other small pasta shapes

1 zucchini, trimmed and diced

Salt and freshly ground pepper

⅓ cup (3 fl oz/80 ml) pesto, homemade (page 215) or purchased

3-oz (90-g) piece Parmesan cheese

2 tablespoons small fresh basil leaves

MAKES 6–8 SERVINGS

In a large bowl, combine the beans with water to cover by 2 inches (5 cm) and let soak overnight. Drain well.

In a large, heavy frying pan over medium-high heat, warm the oil. Add the onion, carrots, and celery and sauté until softened and beginning to brown, about 6 minutes. Stir in the garlic and oregano and cook for about 1 minute more. Pour in 1 cup (8 fl oz/250 ml) of the stock and stir to dislodge any browned bits on the pan bottom. Transfer the contents of the pan to a slow cooker and stir in the drained beans, the remaining 4 cups (32 fl oz/1 l) stock, the tomatoes, and the cheese rind, if using. Cover and cook on the low setting for about 6 hours. The beans should be tender.

Stir in the pasta, zucchini, ½ teaspoon salt, and several grinds of pepper, re-cover, and cook for 30 minutes more. The beans should be very tender and the pasta should be al dente.

Remove and discard the cheese rind, if using. Using the back of a spoon, mash some of the beans against the inside of the slow cooker to thicken the soup a little, then mix together well.

Ladle the soup into warm shallow bowls. Top each serving with a spoonful of the pesto. Using a vegetable peeler, shave the Parmesan over the top. Sprinkle with the basil leaves and serve at once.

After you grate the last bit of cheese from a wedge of Parmesan, save the rind in the freezer. It will add deep flavor to many soups or stews. If you don't have time to make your own pesto, choose a pesto in the refrigerated section of the market for the best flavor.

Creamy Herbed Polenta with Mushrooms

4 cups (32 fl oz/1 l) chicken stock, homemade (page 214) or purchased

1 cup (7 oz/220 g) stone-ground polenta

Salt and freshly ground pepper

1 tablespoon unsalted butter

1 tablespoon olive oil

1 large shallot, finely chopped

¾ lb (375 g) cremini mushrooms, brushed clean and quartered

3 cloves garlic, minced

2 tablespoons coarsely chopped fresh flat-leaf parsley

2 teaspoons *each* minced fresh oregano and minced fresh thyme, plus more for garnish

½ cup (2 oz/60 g) grated Parmesan cheese

1 cup (6 oz/185 g) fresh or thawed, frozen corn kernels

MAKES 4–6 SERVINGS

In a slow cooker, stir together the stock, polenta, 1 teaspoon salt, and several grinds of pepper. Cover and cook on the low setting for 3 to 3½ hours, stirring two or three times if possible. The liquid should be absorbed and the polenta should be thick and soft and no longer gritty.

About 10 minutes before the polenta is ready, in a large, heavy saucepan over medium-high heat, melt the butter with the oil. Add the shallot and mushrooms and cook, stirring frequently, until the mushrooms are tender and their liquid has evaporated, about 5 minutes. Stir in the garlic and parsley, season with salt and pepper, and cook for 1 minute more.

About 5 minutes before the polenta is ready, stir in the 2 teaspoons each oregano and thyme, Parmesan, and corn kernels, then re-cover.

Spoon the polenta into warm shallow bowls or a serving bowl and top with the mushroom mixture. Garnish the polenta and mushrooms with more oregano and thyme and serve at once.

A topping of garlicky, earthy mushrooms adds both texture and sharp flavor to creamy, soft polenta laced with sweet corn kernels. Because polenta cooks unattended in a slow cooker—there's no need for the typical constant stirring—you can serve it alongside a main course that requires last-minute attention, such as grilled or panfried veal or lamb chops.

Artichoke Risotto

3 tablespoons unsalted butter

2 tablespoons olive oil

2 large shallots, finely chopped

8 cloves garlic, sliced

2 cups (14 oz/440 g) Arborio or Carnaroli rice

1 cup (8 fl oz/250 ml) dry white wine

6 cups (48 fl oz/1.5 l) vegetable or chicken stock, homemade (page 214–215) or purchased

Salt and freshly ground pepper

8 oz (250 g) frozen artichoke hearts, thawed and halved lengthwise

Herbed Mushroom Salad for serving (see note; optional)

¼ cup (1 oz/30 g) grated Parmesan cheese

MAKES 4 SERVINGS

In a large frying pan over medium-high heat, melt 1 tablespoon of the butter with the oil. Add the shallots and sauté until lightly golden, about 6 minutes. Add the garlic and cook for 1 minute more. Add the rice, stir to coat with the fat, and cook, stirring, until the rice kernels start to click on the pan, 1–2 minutes. Add the wine and simmer, stirring occasionally, until it has been almost completely absorbed, about 5 minutes. Stir in 1 cup (8 fl oz/250 ml) of the stock, then transfer the contents of the pan to a slow cooker. Add 1 teaspoon salt and the remaining 5 cups (40 fl oz/1.25 l) stock. Cover and cook on the high setting for 1 hour.

Add the artichokes, re-cover, and continue to cook for 1¼ hours longer. The rice should be tender but slightly al dente in the center and the mixture creamy. Stir in the remaining 2 tablespoons butter and several grinds of pepper. Taste and adjust the seasoning with salt.

To serve, spoon the risotto into warm shallow bowls. Top each serving with some of the salad, if using. Sprinkle the Parmesan over the top and serve at once.

ADD FRESHNESS WITH **HERBED MUSHROOM SALAD** Brush clean ½ lb (250 g) fresh white mushrooms or cremini mushrooms, trim the stems, and cut the mushrooms vertically into paper-thin slices. Place the sliced mushrooms in a bowl and add ⅓ cup (3 fl oz/80 ml) Parsley Vinaigrette (page 216). Toss gently until lightly coated.

Farro with Spring Vegetables

3 tablespoons olive oil

½ yellow onion, finely chopped

2 stalks celery, finely chopped

1 oz (30 g) pancetta, finely chopped

1½ cups (10½ oz/330 g) farro, rinsed

½ cup (4 fl oz/125 ml) dry white wine

4 cups (32 fl oz/1 l) chicken stock, homemade (page 214) or purchased

Salt and freshly ground pepper

1 bunch asparagus, about 1 lb (500 g)

1 tablespoon unsalted butter

2 leeks, including the light green tops, cut into matchsticks

2 cups (10 oz/315 g) fresh or thawed, frozen English peas

Grated zest and juice of ½ lemon

2 tablespoons chopped fresh flat-leaf parsley

3-oz (90-g) piece Parmesan cheese

MAKES 6 SERVINGS

In a large, heavy frying pan over medium heat, warm 2 tablespoons of the oil. Add the onion, celery, and pancetta and sauté until the onion is softened and the pancetta has rendered most of its fat, about 5 minutes. Add the farro and stir to coat with the oil. Cook, stirring, until lightly toasted, 1–2 minutes. Add the wine and stir until it has evaporated, about 5 minutes. Pour in 1 cup (8 fl oz/250 ml) of the stock and stir to dislodge any browned bits on the pan bottom. Transfer the contents of the pan to a slow cooker. Stir in the remaining 3 cups (24 fl oz/750 ml) stock, ¼ teaspoon salt, and several grinds of pepper. Cover and cook on the low setting for 2–2½ hours. The farro should be tender.

While the farro is cooking, trim the tough stem ends from the asparagus and then cut the spears into 2-inch (5-cm) lengths. Bring a saucepan three-fourths full of salted water to a boil, add all the asparagus pieces except the tips, and cook for 4 minutes. Add the asparagus tips and cook until all the pieces are tender-crisp, about 2 minutes longer. Drain and run under cold running water until cool. Spread on a kitchen towel to dry.

About 5 minutes before the farro is ready, in a large, heavy frying pan over medium heat, melt the butter with the remaining 1 tablespoon oil. Add the leeks and sauté for 1 minute. Add the peas and sauté for 1 minute. Add the asparagus and sauté until all the vegetables are just tender and heated through, 1–2 minutes. Stir in the lemon juice.

Stir the vegetables into the farro and transfer to a warm serving dish. Garnish with the lemon zest and parsley. Using a vegetable peeler, shave the Parmesan over the top. Serve at once.

Farro, an ancient strain of wheat popular in Italian kitchens, holds its shape beautifully as it cooks, making it ideal for salads, side dishes, and soups. Here, it is tossed together with peas, leeks, and asparagus in a colorful and healthy dish that is perfect with grilled poultry or meat.

Polenta with Cheese, Garlic & Chard

4 cups (32 fl oz/1 l) chicken stock, homemade (page 214) or purchased

1 cup (7 oz/220 g) stone-ground polenta

Salt and freshly ground pepper

1 bunch Swiss chard

2 tablespoons olive oil

3 cloves garlic, finely chopped

1 cup (6 oz/185 g) cherry tomatoes, halved

½ cup (2 oz/60 g) grated Parmesan cheese

¼ lb (125 g) fontina cheese, cut into cubes

3 tablespoons pine nuts, toasted (page 217) and coarsely chopped

MAKES 4–6 SERVINGS

In a slow cooker, stir together the stock, polenta, 1 teaspoon salt, and several grinds of pepper. Cover and cook on the low setting for 3 to 3½ hours, stirring two or three times if possible. The liquid should be absorbed and the polenta should be thick and soft and no longer gritty.

About 20 minutes before the polenta is ready, cut off the stems from the chard leaves. Chop the chard stems crosswise into small pieces. Cut the leaves crosswise about 1 inch (2.5 cm) wide. In a large, heavy saucepan over medium heat, warm the oil. Add the chard stems and cook, stirring occasionally, until beginning to soften, about 8 minutes. Add the garlic, cherry tomatoes, and chard leaves and season well with salt and pepper. Stir well, cover the pan, and cook until the leaves are wilted and tender, 4–5 minutes more.

About 5 minutes before the polenta is ready, stir in the Parmesan and dot the top with the fontina, then re-cover.

Spoon the polenta into warm shallow bowls and top with the chard mixture. Scatter the pine nuts over the top. Serve at once.

If you've never cooked polenta because you are put off by the constant stirring required, this slow-cooker version solves the problem. Topping the polenta with a sautéed mixture of chard and cherry tomatoes delivers fresh flavors and transforms it into a comforting one-bowl meal.

Wild Rice with Red Cabbage Slaw

1 tablespoon unsalted butter

3 tablespoons olive oil

½ yellow onion, finely chopped

2 stalks celery, finely chopped

1 carrot, peeled and finely chopped

½ cup (4 fl oz/125 ml) medium-dry sherry

1¼ cups (8 oz/250 g) wild rice

3 cups (24 fl oz/750 ml) vegetable or chicken stock, homemade (page 214–215) or purchased

Salt and freshly ground pepper

½ lb (250 g) red cabbage, tough outer leaves removed

1 large shallot, finely chopped

1 tablespoon mayonnaise

1 teaspoon Dijon mustard

1 tablespoon cider vinegar

1 cup (6 oz/185 g) dried currants or raisins

¾ cup (3 oz/90 g) walnut pieces, toasted (page 217)

MAKES 4–6 SERVINGS

Oil a slow-cooker insert. In a large, heavy frying pan over medium-high heat, melt the butter with 1 tablespoon of the oil. Add the onion, celery, and carrot and sauté until softened and beginning to brown, about 6 minutes. Pour in the sherry and stir to dislodge any browned bits on the pan bottom. Transfer the contents of the pan to the slow cooker.

Stir in the wild rice, stock, ¼ teaspoon salt, and several grinds of pepper. Cover and cook on the low setting for 2–3 hours. The rice kernels should have just begun to burst but still have some texture when you bite into them.

About 1 hour before serving, to make the slaw, core the red cabbage and finely shred. In a large bowl, whisk together the shallot, mayonnaise, mustard, vinegar, and the remaining 2 tablespoons oil. Add the cabbage, currants, and walnuts and toss to coat evenly. Set aside.

Using a slotted spoon, divide the wild rice among warm individual plates. Top each serving with a spoonful of the slaw. Serve at once.

The cooking time for wild rice can be unpredictable, which is why a range is given here. It is important that you not overcook wild rice, as once the kernels burst, they quickly become mushy. Here, its naturally nutty flavor and chewy texture is paired with a richly textured slaw.

Tuscan Bean Soup

1 cup (7 oz/220 g) dried cranberry beans, picked over and rinsed

3 tablespoons olive oil

1 large onion, finely chopped

3 carrots, peeled, halved lengthwise, and cut into chunks

2 stalks celery, finely chopped

6 cloves garlic, sliced

6 cups (48 fl oz/1.5 l) vegetable or chicken stock, homemade (page 214–215) or purchased

2 sprigs fresh oregano

1 cup (7 oz/220 g) farro, rinsed

1 can (15 oz/470 g) diced tomatoes, drained

2 teaspoons balsamic vinegar

Salt and freshly ground pepper

6 oz (185 g) thickly sliced pancetta, chopped

1½ cups (1½ oz/45 g) baby spinach or arugula

Shredded Parmesan cheese for serving

MAKES 4–6 SERVINGS

In a large bowl, combine the beans with water to cover by 2 inches (5 cm) and let soak overnight. Drain well.

In a large, heavy frying pan over medium-high heat, warm 2 tablespoons of the oil. Add the onion, carrots, and celery and sauté until beginning to brown, 5–6 minutes. Add the garlic and cook for 1 minute more. Pour in 1 cup (8 fl oz/250 ml) of the stock and stir to dislodge any browned bits on the pan bottom. Transfer the contents of the pan to a slow cooker. Stir in the drained beans, the remaining 5 cups (40 fl oz/1.25 l) stock, and the oregano. Cover and cook on the low setting for 4 hours.

Stir in the farro, tomatoes, vinegar, ½ teaspoon salt, and several grinds of pepper, re-cover, and cook for 2 hours more. The beans should be tender but not mushy and the farro should be tender but still slightly firm.

About 5 minutes before the soup is ready, in a heavy frying pan over medium heat, warm the remaining 1 tablespoon oil and add the pancetta. Sauté, stirring frequently, until the pancetta is crisp and golden, about 4 minutes. Using a slotted spoon, transfer to paper towels to drain.

Remove and discard the oregano sprigs from the soup. Ladle the soup into warm shallow bowls. Top each serving with some of the spinach. Garnish with the Parmesan and pancetta and serve at once.

A perfect winter dish, this soup is at once light and comforting. It calls for farro, a grain that boasts a chewy, firm texture when cooked. Arugula or spinach is stirred into the soup just before serving, releasing its earthy flavor, while a garnish of crisp bits of pancetta and curls of Parmesan adds the perfect amount of both texture and saltiness.

Basic Recipes

Beef Stock

2½ lb (1.25 kg) beef marrow bones

1½ lb (750 g) meaty beef bones such as shank, neck, or rib

1 tablespoon canola oil

1 yellow onion, coarsely chopped

1 carrot, coarsely chopped

1 stalk celery with leaves, chopped

8 sprigs fresh flat-leaf parsley

4 sprigs fresh thyme, or ½ teaspoon dried thyme

¼ teaspoon peppercorns

2 bay leaves

Preheat the oven to 425°F (220°C). Spread all of the beef bones in a roasting pan just large enough to hold them in a single layer. Roast until the bones are nicely browned, about 40 minutes.

Just before the bones are ready, in a stockpot, heat the oil over medium-high heat. Add the onion, carrot, and celery and cook, stirring occasionally, until lightly browned, about 5 minutes. Remove from the heat.

When the bones are ready, transfer them to the stockpot. Pour out and discard the fat from the roasting pan, then place the pan over high heat. Pour in 2 cups water, bring to a boil, and stir to dislodge any browned bits on the pan bottom. Pour the contents of the pan into the stockpot and add cold water to cover the bones by 1 inch (2.5 cm); you will need about 3 qt (3 l). Bring just to a boil over high heat, skimming off any foam that rises to the surface. Add the parsley, thyme, peppercorns, and bay leaves, reduce the heat to low, and simmer gently, uncovered, continuing to skim any foam that rises to the surface, until the stock is full flavored, at least 3 hours or up to 5 hours. Add more water to the pot as needed to keep the bones covered.

Remove the pot from the heat and remove and discard the bones. Strain the stock through a colander set over a large heatproof bowl. Discard the solids in the colander. Let the stock stand for 5 minutes, then skim off the fat from the surface. Use the stock at once or let cool to room temperature, cover, and refrigerate for up to 3 days or freeze for up to 3 months. Lift off and discard the fat congealed on the surface before using.

MAKES ABOUT 2 QT (2 L)

Chicken Stock

5 lb (2.5 kg) chicken backs and necks

2 carrots, coarsely chopped

1 leek, including about 6 inches (15 cm) of the green tops, coarsely chopped

1 celery stalk, coarsely chopped

4 sprigs fresh flat-leaf parsley

2 sprigs fresh thyme, or ½ teaspoon dried thyme

¼ teaspoon peppercorns

In a stockpot, combine the chicken parts, carrots, leek, celery, parsley, thyme, and peppercorns. Add cold water to cover by 1 inch (2.5 cm). Place the pot over medium-high heat and bring almost to a boil. Using a large spoon, skim off any scum and froth from the surface. Reduce the heat to low and simmer uncovered, skimming the surface as needed and adding more water if necessary to keep the ingredients immersed, until the meat has fallen off the bones and the stock is flavorful and fragrant, about 3 hours.

Remove from the heat and and strain the stock through a colander set over a large heatproof bowl. Discard the solids in the colander. Let the stock stand for 5 minutes, then skim off the fat from the surface. Use the stock at once or let cool to room temperature, cover, and refrigerate for up to 3 days or freeze for up to 3 months. Lift off and discard the fat congealed on the surface before using.

MAKES ABOUT 3 QT (3 L)

Vegetable Stock

3 large leeks

2 yellow onions, coarsely chopped

4 carrots, coarsely chopped

3 stalks celery with leaves, chopped

¼ lb (125 g) fresh button mushrooms, brushed clean and halved

6 sprigs fresh flat-leaf parsley

2 sprigs fresh thyme, or ½ teaspoon dried thyme

¼ teaspoon peppercorns

Trim, halve, and rinse the leeks, then cut into chunks. In a stockpot, combine the leeks, onions, carrots, celery, mushrooms, parsley, thyme, and peppercorns. Add about 2 qt (2 l) water to the stockpot and bring to a boil over high heat. Reduce the heat to medium-low, cover partially, and simmer until the vegetables are very soft and the flavors have blended, about 1 hour.

Remove from the heat and and strain the stock through a colander set over a large heatproof bowl. Press down on the solids to extract all the liquid, and discard the solids. Use the stock at once or let cool to room temperature, cover, and refrigerate for up to 3 days or freeze for up to 3 months.

MAKES ABOUT 2 QT (2 L)

Fish Stock

2½ lb (1.25 kg) fish bones, heads, and skin, rinsed

1 large yellow onion, coarsely chopped

½ fennel bulb, trimmed and coarsely chopped

3 celery stalks, coarsely chopped

1 carrot, peeled and chopped

1 leek, including tender green parts, chopped

2 cups (16 fl oz/500 ml) dry white wine

In a stockpot, combine the fish parts, onion, fennel, celery, carrot, leek, wine, and 6 cups (48 fl oz/1.5 l) cold water. Place the pot over medium-high heat and slowly bring almost to a boil. Using a large spoon,

skim off any scum and froth from the surface. Reduce the heat to low and simmer uncovered, skimming the surface as needed, until the flesh starts to fall off the bones and the stock is fragrant and flavorful, about 25 minutes.

Remove from the heat and and strain the stock through a colander set over a large heatproof bowl. Discard the solids in the colander. Use the stock at once or let cool to room temperature, cover, and refrigerate for up to 3 days or freeze for up to 3 months.

MAKES ABOUT 2 QT (2 L)

Pesto

2½ cups (2½ oz/75 g) fresh basil leaves

3 garlic cloves, coarsely chopped

3 tablespoons pine nuts, lightly toasted (page 217)

¾ cup (6 fl oz/180 ml) extra-virgin olive oil

Salt

¼ cup (1 oz/30 g) grated Parmesan cheese

In a food processor, combine the basil, garlic, pine nuts, oil, and ⅛ teaspoon salt and process until blended and nearly smooth, about 30 seconds. Add the Parmesan and blend for 5 seconds more.

Use at once, or transfer to a jar, pour a thin layer of oil on top, cover tightly, and refrigerate for up to 1 week.

MAKES ABOUT 1½ CUPS (12 FL OZ/375 ML)

Horseradish Mayonnaise

½ cup (4 fl oz/125 ml) mayonnaise

3 tablespoons plain yogurt or sour cream

2 tablespoons prepared horseradish

1 tablespoon Dijon mustard

½ teaspoon Worcestershire sauce

In a bowl, whisk together the mayonnaise, yogurt, horseradish, mustard, and Worcestershire sauce. Use immediately, or cover and refrigerate for up to 1 week.

MAKES ABOUT ¾ CUP (6 FL OZ/180 ML)

Parsley Vinaigrette

1 teaspoon Dijon mustard

3 tablespoons red wine vinegar

Salt and freshly ground pepper

¼ cup (2 fl oz/60 ml) extra-virgin olive oil

1 tablespoon finely chopped fresh flat-leaf parsley

In a small bowl, whisk together the mustard, vinegar, ¼ teaspoon salt, and a few grinds of pepper. Whisk in the oil until emulsified. Stir in the parsley.

MINT VINAIGRETTE Substitute 1 tablespoon finely chopped fresh mint for the parsley.

DILL VINAIGRETTE Substitute 2 tablespoons finely chopped fresh dill for the parsley.

MAKES ABOUT ½ CUP (4 FL OZ/125 ML)

Lemon Vinaigrette

1 teaspoon Dijon mustard

1 tablespoon white wine vinegar

1 teaspoon finely grated lemon zest

2 tablespoons fresh lemon juice

Salt and freshly ground pepper

¼ cup (2 fl oz/6o ml) extra-virgin olive oil

In a small bowl, whisk together the mustard, vinegar, lemon zest and juice, ½ teaspoon salt, and a few grinds of pepper. Whisk in the oil until emulsified.

LIME VINAIGRETTE Substitute 1 teaspoon finely grated lime zest for the lemon zest and 2 tablespoons fresh lime juice for the lemon juice.

ORANGE VINAIGRETTE Substitute 1 teaspoon finely grated orange zest for the lemon zest and 2 tablespoons fresh orange juice for the lemon juice.

MAKES ABOUT ½ CUP (4 FL OZ/125 ML)

Asian Lime Vinaigrette

2 tablespoons extra-virgin olive oil

1 tablespoon low-sodium soy sauce

Juice of 1 lime

2 teaspoons sherry vinegar

1 teaspoon peeled and minced fresh ginger

⅛ teaspoon sugar

2 or 3 drops Tabasco or other hot pepper sauce

Salt

In a blender or mini food processor, combine the oil, soy sauce, lime juice, vinegar, ginger, sugar, Tabasco to taste, and ⅛ teaspoon salt and process for 15 seconds.

MAKES ABOUT ½ CUP (4 FL OZ/125 ML)

Shallot Vinaigrette

1 teaspoon Dijon mustard

1 small shallot, minced

3 tablespoons red wine vinegar

Salt and freshly ground pepper

¼ cup (2 fl oz/60 ml) extra-virgin olive oil

In a small bowl, whisk together the mustard, shallot, vinegar, ¼ teaspoon salt, and a few grinds of pepper. Whisk in the oil until emulsified.

MAKES ABOUT ½ CUP (4 FL OZ/125 ML)

Crostini

Baguette slices, about 2 inches (5 cm) in diameter and ½ inch (12 mm) thick

Extra-virgin olive oil for brushing

1–2 garlic cloves, halved lengthwise

Preheat the oven to 350°F (180°C). Arrange the baguette slices on a rimmed baking sheet and brush lightly with olive oil. Bake until golden, 10–15 minutes. Carefully rub each baguette slice on one side with a cut side of the garlic clove while still warm.

Basic Techniques

Zesting Citrus

The best tool for zesting citrus is a fine-rasp Microplane grater. Hold the citrus fruit in the palm of one hand over a bowl and pull the grater across the fruit with the other hand, following the contour of the fruit and removing only the colored portion of the rind. Take care not to include the bitter white pith that lies just underneath. Tap the grater firmly on the side of the bowl to release the zest. If you don't have a Microplane or other fine-rasp grater, remove the zest with a vegetable peeler and then finely mince the zest with a sharp knife.

Segmenting Citrus

Cut a slice off the top and the bottom of the fruit to reveal the flesh. Stand the fruit upright and, following its contour, slice downward, removing the peel and pith in wide strips. Holding the fruit over a bowl to catch the juice, cut along both sides of each segment to release it from the membrane. If needed, use the tip of the knife to dislodge any seeds. Use the segments whole or cut as directed in individual recipes.

Trimming Baby Artichokes

Fill a bowl three-fourths full with cold water. Squeeze in the juice of ½ lemon. Working with one artichoke at a time, peel away any tough outer leaves. Using a paring knife or kitchen scissors, trim about ¼ inch (6 mm) off the top of the artichoke. Trim the tips of any leaves with thorny tips. Trim the stem. Cut the artichoke in half lengthwise and, using a teaspoon, scoop out the fuzzy choke, if any, covering the heart. Drop each artichoke into the lemon water, which will slow discoloration.

Cleaning Leeks

Trim the dark green leaves off the top of the leek. Reserve for adding to stock or discard. Cut the leek in half lengthwise, keeping the root intact if using the leek whole. Rinse under cold running water, gently holding the layers open to rinse away dirt trapped between them. Cut or slice as directed in individual recipes.

Toasting Nuts and Coconut

Preheat the oven to 325°F (165°C). Spread the nuts or shredded dried coconut in a single layer on a small rimmed baking sheet and toast, stirring occasionally for even browning, until fragrant and the color deepens, 5–10 minutes for the coconut or 10–20 minutes for the nuts. The timing for the nuts depends on their type and size; check regularly to avoid burning.

Skinning Nuts

To skin hazelnuts, peanuts, or walnuts, toast the nuts as directed for toasting nuts. Pour the still-warm nuts into a coarse-textured kitchen towel and rub vigorously to remove the skins. Peel away any stubborn skins with your fingers; don't worry if tiny bits remain. To skin almonds or pistachios, place the nuts in a heatproof bowl, add boiling water to cover, and let stand for 1 minute. Drain, rinse with cold running water, and drain again. Squeeze each nut between two fingers to remove the skin.

Index

weldon**owen**

415 Jackson Street, Suite 200, San Francisco, CA 94111
Telephone: 415 291 0100 Fax: 415 291 8841
www.weldonowen.com

A DIVISION OF
BONNIER

THE NEW SLOW COOKER

Conceived and produced by Weldon Owen, Inc.
in collaboration with Williams-Sonoma, Inc.
3250 Van Ness Avenue, San Francisco, CA 94109

Photographer Kate Sears
Food Stylist Robyn Valarik
Prop Stylist Sara Slavin

Additional photography:
Ray Kachatorian, page 11;
Petrina Tinslay, page 7;
Tucker and Hossler, pages 7, 16

Printed and bound by 1010 Printing International, Ltd., China

This edition first printed in 2013
10 9 8 7 6 5 4 3 2

Library of Congress Cataloging-in-Publication data is available.

ISBN-13: 978-1-61628-602-6
ISBN-10: 1-61628-602-4

ACKNOWLEDGMENTS

Weldon Owen would like to thank the following people for their generous support in making this book:
Leslie Evans, Lauren Grant, Ashley Lima, Rachel Lopez Metzger, Elizabeth Parson,
Sharon Silva, Victoria Wall, Jason Wheeler, and Tracy White.